THE ESSENTIAL
ROSE
GARDEN

THE ESSENTIAL
ROSE
GARDEN

A PRACTICAL GUIDE TO GROWING,
CARE AND MAINTENANCE OF ROSES

PETER McHOY

HERMES
HOUSE

This edition published in the US in 1998 by Hermes House
27 West 20th Street, New York, NY 10011

HERMES HOUSE books are available for bulk
purchase for sales promotion and for premium
use. For details, write or call the
sales director, Hermes House,
27 West 20th Street, New York,
NY 10011; (800) 354-9657

Hermes House is an imprint of
Anness Publishing Limited

ISBN 1 84038 071 3

Publisher: Joanna Lorenz
Editorial Manager: Helen Sudell
Designer: Bet Ayer

Previously published as part of a larger compendium, *The Ultimate Rose Book*

The publishers would like to credit Peter McHoy and John Freeman for photographs used in this book

Printed in Singapore by Star Standard Industries Pte. Ltd.

3 5 7 9 10 8 6 4 2

Contents

A HISTORY OF THE ROSE

The rose has been a significant symbol for centuries. Probably a native of the northern hemisphere, it has been carried by settlers all over the world, where it has adapted and flourished. Now the world's most beloved flower, this remarkably varied species has a rich and colourful history.

𝒜 HISTORY OF THE ROSE

Prized, cherished and fought over for centuries, roses now grow all over the world, although they are almost certainly indigenous to the northern hemisphere. Rose fossils, millions of years old, have been found only north of the equator, suggesting that those species now growing in South Africa, South America, Australia and New Zealand were taken there by emigrants.

ANCIENT ROSES

The wild rose was most certainly enjoyed by early people for its sweet petals and tasty hips, and rose cultivation probably began around 5,000 years ago in China and in what is now Iraq. In the *Iliad*, Homer's epic composed around 1200 BC, the poet tells of Achilles' shield being decorated with roses to celebrate his victory over Hector. Hector's body was anointed with rose oil before it was embalmed.

The roses mentioned by many Greek historians were almost certainly *Rosa gallica*, the ancestor of numerous European roses. Known as the 'Apothecary's Rose' or 'Red Damask', *R. g. officinalis* was the main source of rose oil and medicinal remedies in Europe until the introduction of rose species from the Far East.

The early Christian church condemned roses as a symbol of depravity, with some justification since Nero's obsession with these

PREVIOUS PAGE: 'Rosa '*Duchesse de Montebello*'.

flowers almost certainly contributed to the fall of the Roman Empire. The emperor's excesses were notorious and it is said that tons of roses were required for the numerous banquets he gave where guests sat on pillows stuffed with them. Vast quantities of petals were showered over people at orgies, reputedly suffocating at least one participant, and pure rose-water baths were offered to all the guests.

Roses symbolized success in Roman times and millions of petals were threaded on to brass wires to make garlands and headdresses. Peasants consequently came to believe that it was more profitable to grow roses than corn, a disastrous misconception noted by the Roman poet Horace and other intellectuals of his time.

ABOVE: A descendant of the ancient gallica roses 'Cardinal de Richelieu' is a sumptuous purple rose raised in France in 1840.

BELOW: One of the best-known and most ancient of all historic roses, R. gallica officinalis, the 'Apothecary's Rose' or 'Red Damask', was widely grown for its scent in the Middle Ages.

THE MIDDLE AGES

Little information exists about the cultivation of roses following the collapse of the Roman Empire until about AD 400, when the church adopted the white *R. alba* as the emblem of the Virgin Mary.

In 1272 Edward I of England, upon his return from the last Crusade, ordered rose trees to be planted in the gardens of the Tower of London and chose a gold rose as his own symbol.

It is possible that returning Crusaders were responsible for the introduction of *R. damascena*. Certainly by the end of the fifteenth century the rose 'Autumn Damask', known in France as 'Quatre Saisons'

and the first rose in Europe to produce two crops of flowers every summer, was growing in English gardens.

It is debatable whether *R. gallica* was brought to England by the Romans or at a later date by returning Crusaders. It was, however, the emblem of the House of Lancaster in the prolonged struggle against the house of York (who adopted *R.* x *alba*) during the bitter Wars of the Roses in England in the fifteenth century.

The marriage of Henry Tudor (Henry VII) and Elizabeth of York finally united the factions. Their emblem was a white rose in the centre of a red rose entwined with a crown. Since then the British royal family have adopted the rose as their own.

By the end of the sixteenth century, *R. foetida* had been introduced into Europe from what was then Persia and *R. moschata*, the musk rose, was certainly favoured by the court of Henry VIII.

ABOVE: Rosa gallica versicolor *or 'Rosa Mundi' is a striped sport from* R. g. officinalis *first recorded in 1581.*

European roses were taken to America by the Pilgrim Fathers and by the beginning of the seventeenth century were growing in many gardens in Massachusetts. North America already had its own species, *R. virginiana* and *R. carolina*. Another, *R. setigera*, would later produce some vigorous rambler cultivars including the pale pink 'Baltimore Belle', still famous in America, and the climber 'Long John Silver', a fragrant pure white.

EARLY HYBRIDS

Until the process of hybridization was understood in the nineteenth century, new rose varieties were the results of natural crosses or sports (mutations), carefully chosen and nurtured by gardeners and nurserymen. Dutch breeders pioneered work in Europe in the seventeenth century, working on *R. centifolia*, or the Provence Rose,

ABOVE: *'Old Blush', now more correctly called* R. x odorata *'Pallida', is one of the original China roses. Its scent and long flowering season ensure that it is still planted by rose lovers.*

ABOVE: *'Little White Pet' (1879) is a dwarf shrub which originated in the USA as a sport of the vigorous rambler 'Félicité et Perpétue'.*

also known as the cabbage rose because of its "hundred-leaved" flowers. Moss roses appeared around the mid-eighteenth century as a sport (mutation) from *R. centifolia*.

Rose breeding was given tremendous impetus by the patronage of the Empress Josephine, wife of Napoleon. Between 1803 and 1814 she commissioned botanists and nurserymen all over the world to discover and breed new roses for her garden at Malmaison near Paris, where she eventually grew over 250 varieties.

INTRODUCTIONS FROM THE FAR EAST

The Chinese had been growing roses for thousands of years, and these began to reach European growers in the late eighteenth century. Around 1781 a pink rose, *R. chinensis*, now known as 'Old Blush', was planted in the Netherlands and soon came to

England. Some years later a captain of the British East India Company returned home with a red form of the same rose, which he had found growing in Calcutta, and it was named *R. semperflorens*, the 'Bengal Rose', or 'Slater's Crimson China'. Between them, these two roses are responsible for the remontant or repeat-flowering qualities in most modern roses.

At the beginning of the nineteenth century the flowers known as tea roses arrived on the ships of the British East India Company – their main cargo was tea, which probably accounts for the common name of these roses. They became fashionable in Europe, but because many of them are tender the Victorians grew them in grand conservatories, along with other exotic flowers brought back by explorers and botanists from all parts of the British empire.

ABOVE: 'Madame Alfred Carrière', a Noisette climber raised in 1879, is still widely grown in gardens and is especially valued because it will grow successfully on a north-facing wall.

ABOVE: 'Souvenir de la Malmaison', a famous old Bourbon rose, has beautiful quartered flowers in soft powder pink. There is a climbing as well as a bush form.

EAST MEETS WEST

One of the first marriages between a rose from the West and one from the East was a cross between 'Autumn Damask' and a red China rose which was probably obtained from France by the second Duchess of Portland, an enthusiastic rose collector of the late eighteenth century. The Portland roses, as they became known, were very popular in the early 1800s. Though few survive today, they are ideal for growing in containers and are prized for their perfume and ability to flower throughout the summer.

Meanwhile, at around the same time in Charleston, South Carolina, a rice-grower called John Champneys crossed a musk rose, *R. moschata*, with a China rose, *R. chinensis* 'Parson's Pink China' or 'Old Blush', which had been a gift from his friend and neighbour, Philippe Noisette. He gave the new seedling to Noisette, who made more crosses and sent both seed and plants to his brother Louis in Paris. The first seedlings he called 'Rosier de Philippe Noisette', a long name that inevitably came to be shortened to 'Noisette'.

'Blush Noisette' is still widely grown today and so too is the beautiful 'Madame Alfred Carrière', one of the few climbing roses that can tolerate a north-facing wall.

Bourbon roses also made their appearance during this period. These began as a cross between 'Old Blush' and 'Autumn Damask' found growing in rose hedges on the Ile de Bourbon in the Indian Ocean. Many of these shrub roses are still available, including 'Louise Odier', 'Souvenir de la Malmaison' and the much-prized, thornless 'Zéphirine Drouhin'.

ABOVE: The beautiful Bourbon climber 'Zéphirine Drouhin' dates from 1868 and is greatly valued for its virtually thornless stems and long flowering season.

THE MODERN ROSE

Throughout the nineteenth century hybrid perpetuals were introduced as a result of breeding between Chinas, Portlands, Bourbons and Noisettes.

The birth of what is considered to be the first modern rose, the large-flowered or hybrid tea rose, took place in 1867 with the introduction of Jean-Baptiste Guillot's 'La France'. This new breed of roses satisfied gardeners' demands for neat, repeat-flowering and truly hardy shrubs with elegant and delicate flowers.

In the mid-eighteenth century a wild rambler, *R. multiflora*, had been introduced from Japan. In the hands of nineteenth-century breeders, it was to become the parent of the numerous cluster-flowered or floribunda roses of today.

Most rose-breeders of the twentieth century have concentrated their efforts on floribunda and hybrid tea roses, in colours echoing current tastes in fashion. Since the late 1960s there has been a steady increase in the number of smaller shrubs for tiny gardens, patios and pots.

At the same time, a new breed of roses, evocative of Dutch old masters and the romantic paintings of Pierre-Joseph Redouté, has been introduced by the English rose-grower David Austin. He has raised roses that may be described as some of the finest reproductions, growing no more than 1.2 m (4 ft) tall but with all the charm and scent of classic roses of the past, crossing damasks and gallicas with modern shrub roses. Now owners of even the smallest garden may enjoy the delights of roses that the Empress Josephine would have considered for her garden at Malmaison.

ABOVE: 'Graham Thomas' is one of the most popular of the modern shrub roses bred by David Austin in his series of "English" roses. It combines the form and fragrance of an old rose with a pure yellow colouring that nineteenth-century breeders could not achieve.

ABOVE: 'L. D. Braithwaite' is an outstanding modern shrub rose, with all the charm of the old-fashioned roses.

CLASSIFICATION OF ROSES

The long and eventful history of rose breeding means that today's rose lovers can enjoy an enormous variety of beautiful plants. We have come to expect a great deal from roses, and with thoughtful choice and careful cultivation they reward us with glorious flowers from spring until the dark days of winter; scent that fills the summer garden and lingers on in oils, preserves and pot-pourri; and decorative hips, leaves and even thorns. There are forms and styles suitable for nearly every situation, from diminutive patio bushes to huge ramblers cascading in luxurious swags from trees and arbours.

There are several thousand documented roses, including original species and scores of hybrids that have been cultivated during the last four centuries. New rose hybrids are being introduced every year in addition to older hybrids being rediscovered all over the world.

In 1971, the World Federation of Rose Societies reclassified both ancient and modern roses into more clearly defined garden groups. Broadly speaking, the era of the modern rose began in 1867 with the introduction of the first hybrid tea 'La France'. The various wild species form another group, divided into climbing and non-climbing species.

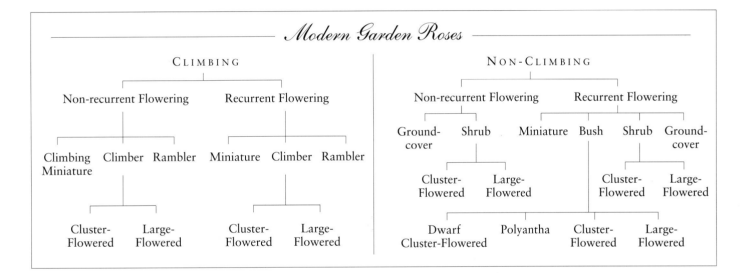

Modern Garden Roses

CLIMBING

Non-recurrent Flowering — Recurrent Flowering

Non-recurrent Flowering: Climbing Miniature, Climber, Rambler
 Climber: Cluster-Flowered, Large-Flowered

Recurrent Flowering: Miniature, Climber, Rambler
 Climber: Cluster-Flowered, Large-Flowered

NON-CLIMBING

Non-recurrent Flowering — Recurrent Flowering

Non-recurrent Flowering: Ground-cover, Shrub
 Shrub: Cluster-Flowered, Large-Flowered

Recurrent Flowering: Miniature, Bush, Shrub, Ground-cover
 Bush: Dwarf Cluster-Flowered, Polyantha, Cluster-Flowered, Large-Flowered
 Shrub: Cluster-Flowered, Large-Flowered

What's in a Name?

Although it is more than 25 years since the new classifications were recommended, both gardeners and growers tend to cling to the old names with which most are familiar. Cluster-flowered roses are still likely to be described as floribundas, and large-flowered roses referred to as hybrid teas, in many catalogues, on labels in rose gardens, and in everyday conversation. For reasons of familiarity the terms "floribunda" and "hybrid tea" have been used freely in this book.

In addition to the "official" categories, catalogues sometimes describe varieties as "patio roses". These are low-growing floribundas suitable for patio beds and even containers. Some of the smallest patio roses are similar in size to the largest of the miniatures.

Catalogues sometimes use a grower's code name for the variety as well as the name under which it is widely known and distributed. For example, 'Sexy Rexy' is the selling name of 'Macrexy' (bred by McGredy), and 'Paul Shirville' is the selling name of 'Harqueterwife' (bred by Harkness). The breeder's name is a way of identifying a variety if the local name is changed when the rose is sold in different countries. It is also the name likely to be used during early trials, before the variety is released to the public.

GROWING BETTER ROSES

This practical section covers how to choose the right rose for your garden and includes step-by-step instructions on how to plant, prune and tend your roses. It also provides a useful year-round breakdown of essential rose care.

$\mathcal{G}$ROWING BETTER ROSES

$\mathcal{R}$oses respond well to a little tender, loving care. If you feed them well and make sure they do not become stressed through lack of water or by pests or diseases, they will reward you for many years with superb displays of beautiful flowers and lush, healthy foliage.

Pruning will also ensure vigorous plants with plenty of blooms. For the best results, however, you do need to know how best to prune each kind of rose and step-by-step instructions on pages 26–37 show how easy and uncomplicated it can be.

Roses are remarkably tough and adaptable, and will go on growing with minimal attention for many years, but they will deteriorate and flower less prolifically, with smaller blooms, on bushes that become poorly shaped. Simple routine care makes an enormous difference, and the benefits will be obvious: lush, compact growth, an abundance of flowers, and blooms and foliage unmarred by pests such as aphids or diseases like mildew.

The regular but simple tasks required during the spring and summer are no hardship to a rose enthusiast. Close regular contact with the plants means that problems are quickly spotted and will seldom become serious. From spring pruning until the first bloom of the season, there is the thrill of anticipation.

PREVIOUS PAGE: Rosa 'Heidi'.

ABOVE: *During the dormant season, bare-root plants are often sold with a wrap to protect their roots. If it is too frosty or wet to plant them, healthy roses can be left in the wrappings for a short time until conditions improve.*

ABOVE: *If you are buying in a shop or garden centre, avoid roses with elongated, new pale shoots, which might indicate long and incorrect storage. This plant has been on sale in the shop for too long.*

ABOVE: *Container-grown roses should have plenty of fine roots around the edge of the root-ball, but not lots of them winding their way around the edge of the pot.*

Frequent close observation shows all the promise of new shoots and then buds growing by the week, with a freshness of foliage which is not matched later in the year.

Working among roses in flower, whether dead-heading or even weeding, is a fragrant and delightful task that brings intimate contact with these most wonderful flowers.

LEFT: Rosa odorata 'Mutabilis' is a China rose of unknown origin, which displays beautifully subtle changes of colour as it ages.

Buying Roses

Roses are sold either container-grown or as bare-root plants (these have been lifted from the field while dormant and the soil shaken off). Bare-root plants sold in shops and garden centres usually have their roots packed in moss or peat, and wrapped in moisture-retaining plastic.

Container-grown plants are available all year round, and can be planted any time the ground is not frozen or waterlogged. Bare-root plants are available only in the dormant season, usually between mid- or late autumn and early spring.

Plants ordered by post from specialist rose nurseries will probably arrive bare-root – testimony to the fact that these plants establish themselves readily if moved when dormant. The quality of bare-root plants from a specialist nursery is usually high and the plants arrive in good condition as they are freshly lifted and have not spent weeks in a shop or garden centre.

RIGHT: When choosing a container-grown rose, look for a plant with a well-balanced basic structure of healthy stems, whether you are buying a ground cover rose (left), when you should see low, horizontal shoots, or a climber (right) with strong upright growth.

PLANTING

A rose is a long-term investment, and will give decades of pleasure if it is looked after. Get it off to a good start with thorough soil preparation and careful planting.

PREPARING THE SOIL

It is a myth that roses only grow well on heavy clay soils: many excellent rose gardens are on light and sandy soils. There is, however, some truth behind the popular belief. Many modern roses tolerate such a wide range of soils only because they are budded on to appropriate rootstocks; plants growing in light and "hungry" soils require more feeding, watering and mulching.

Albas, gallicas, damasks, centifolias, Portlands and moss roses can cope with less fertile soils than modern hybrids, as can species roses such as *R. rugosa* and *R. pimpinellifolia*.

The ideal soil has a pH of around 6.5–7 (slightly acid to neutral). A simple and inexpensive soil test kit will give the pH and instructions for how to modify it if necessary.

Dig over the site to loosen the soil and remove weeds, mixing in as much organic material as possible. Garden compost or well-rotted manure are ideal. If the supply is limited, incorporate it around the root area when planting rather than spreading it thinly while digging. If you find a hard, compacted layer when soil to the depth of a spade's blade has been removed, ensure the ground below is broken up with a fork to improve drainage.

If other roses have previously been growing in the same spot in recent years, remove as much of the old soil as possible and replace it with fresh (or plant your new rose in a different position) to reduce the risk of replant disease.

PLANTING A BARE-ROOT ROSE

1 Dig a hole large enough to take the roots when spread out, and deep enough not to bend them. Incorporate garden compost or well-rotted manure in the base if not already added to the soil when preparing the bed.

2 Work a handful of bonemeal into the planting hole (wear gloves), then spread the roots out evenly, with the plant placed centrally. If the roots grow in just one direction, do not bend them, but plant the rose to one side of the hole.

3 Trickle the soil between the roots, shaking the plant occasionally as the hole is filled to settle the soil. Tread around the base of the plant to firm the soil, and make sure the budding union is completely covered to prevent suckers.

1 Excavate a hole approximately twice the width of the container, and a little deeper. Break up the soil in the bottom with a fork, incorporating humus-forming material such as garden compost or well-rotted manure, if this has not already been done during general preparation of the bed.

2 Remove the rose from its pot, gently tease out some of the roots from around the edge to encourage them to grow out into the surrounding soil, then position the root-ball in the hole. Lay a cane across the hole to check the depth, adding or removing soil as necessary.

3 The graft union (the point where the rose was budded on to its rootstock) should be about 2.5 cm (1 in) below the level of the surrounding bed. Backfill with soil and firm in with your foot to ensure there are no large air pockets where the roots could dry out.

4 If planting in spring or early summer, apply a rose or general garden fertilizer and fork it in lightly. Water well, then mulch with more organic material, such as garden compost or chipped bark, to reduce water evaporation and help suppress weeds.

ROUTINE ROSECARE

Roses respond to care and attention, but especially to feeding, watering and mulching. Simple tasks like dead-heading and removing suckers also improve the appearance of the rose garden as well as ensuring that the plants remain in tip-top condition and bloom prolifically.

FEEDING

Roses are "hungry" shrubs and require feeding if they are to grow to their maximum potential. If any of the important nutrients are deficient, the plant will show symptoms such as weak or stunted growth, small or discoloured leaves and small, poor quality flowers.

Feeding starts at planting time. Plenty of humus-forming material such as garden compost or well-rotted manure adds nutrients as well as improving soil structure. The initial nutrients are soon depleted, but a soil with a high organic content is more likely to retain nutrients that you apply later than, for instance, a light, sandy soil from which fertilizers are quickly leached.

Organic mulches applied annually also help to top up the humus in the soil as they rot down.

It is possible to grow good roses simply by applying plenty of manure or garden compost each year, but for optimum performance an additional boost is required.

Enthusiasts use rose fertilizers that are specially formulated, but where

ABOVE: *Scatter granular or powdered fertilizer in a circle around the base of the plant, but keep it away from the stem.*

ABOVE: *Hoe the fertilizer in so that it penetrates more readily. If it is dry, water in thoroughly.*

just a few roses are grown it may be cheaper or more convenient to use the same general balanced garden fertilizer bought for other flowering plants. Apply the first dose in spring before the leaves open fully, and another one in early or mid-summer when the roses are blooming freely. Follow the instructions on the packet for application rates.

Avoid feeding in late summer as this may encourage the plant to produce soft growth that could be damaged in a cold winter.

Liquid feeding will give roses a useful quick-acting boost, so if other garden plants are being fed from a hose-end dilutor, for example, give the roses a dose if they do not appear to be in tip-top condition.

WATERING

Roses have deep roots, so they do not show signs of water stress until a drought is prolonged, but their growth will probably be impaired, and the flowers smaller.

If water has to be rationed, always give priority to roses planted within the last year. More established bushes are better able to cope with dry soil. Never allow newly planted roses to become dry at the roots.

Try to water thoroughly if there are no restrictions. At any time, one thorough soaking is better than regular dribbles. As a guide, apply 4–5 litres (1 gallon) for a rose bush, three times this for a climber. Water in the evening, when less moisture will be lost through evaporation.

For a large rose bed or border, a permanently installed trickle irrigation hose that can be turned on when required is ideal.

MULCHING

A mulch serves three main purposes: it suppresses weeds, reduces moisture loss through evaporation, and in some cases improves the appearance of the bed.

Plastic mulching sheets are effective, but visually unattractive. They are best used for newly planted roses, and then covered with a thin layer of a more decorative mulch such as chipped bark.

Organic mulches should be applied at least 5 cm (2 in) thick to suppress weeds, when used alone, but should be kept clear of the stems of the roses.

Chipped bark is a popular and efficient mulch, and it looks good. Cocoa shells can also be used, but they may blow about when dry. Rotted manure and garden compost make excellent mulches and add nutrients, but they are not decorative.

ABOVE: *Chipped bark is a widely available mulch and is visually more pleasing than bare soil.*

ABOVE: *Cocoa shells are sometimes used as a mulch. When fresh they are an attractive brown, but this gradually weathers to a more earthy colour.*

Grass clippings can be used as long as a hormone weedkiller has not been used on the grass, but they can look unattractive as they begin to rot.

Spring is the best time to apply a mulch, as the soil is warmed up. Ensure that the ground is moist before mulching.

Organic mulches require topping up occasionally. This is best done in spring or early summer.

LEFT: Strawy manure will help to add plenty of humus to the soil as it slowly rots down, but it is not as attractive as chipped bark.

BELOW: Rotted manure makes an ideal mulch for roses, and it soon blends in with the soil.

DEAD-HEADING

Most roses benefit from dead-heading, especially hybrid teas and floribundas, but do not remove the heads of roses grown for their decorative hips. Removing dead flowers as they fade helps to promote the production of fresh blooms on repeat-flowering roses and improves the appearance of those with a single flush – such as 'Albertine' – whose flowers do not shed their petals and become unsightly as they age.

Although individual flowers can be removed as they fade, this may be too time-consuming if there are many roses in the garden. But at least remove the whole truss when all the blooms have faded, cutting the stem back to the second or third leaf below the flower truss. If the plant is still young, however, do not cut back the stem so hard.

RIGHT: Dead-heading keeps the bushes looking tidy, and it ensures the plant puts most of its energy into producing new growth.

SUCKERS

While dead-heading, keep an eye open for suckers – shoots growing from the rootstock at the base of the plant (or higher up the stem in the case of a standard). Suckers can easily take over the plant and should be removed by pulling each one off at the point of origin. Snipping off the suckers may only encourage more of them to grow.

Suckers look different to the stems of the grafted rose. The leaves may be a different colour, or smaller than those of the variety, and may have seven leaflets instead of five.

1 Remove suckers at their point of origin, which usually involves pulling away some of the soil.

2 If possible, pull them off, otherwise try to cut them off flush with the main stem.

ROSE HEALTHCARE

Roses are popular with pests as well as people. Unfortunately they are prone to pests such as greenfly and diseases like blackspot and mildew, as well as a number of less serious problems. All of these can be controlled, but vigilance is required to nip problems in the bud.

Incidence of disease and pest attack is influenced to some extent by the climate and regional variations: blackspot is more prevalent in some areas than in others, mildew is more likely to be a problem if the weather is damp, and greenfly populations are partly governed by the winter survival of their predators.

Some rose varieties are more susceptible to problems than others, but well-fed roses that are growing strongly usually shake off the effects of any attack more readily, especially if quick action is taken. Avoid introducing pests or disease into your garden by alway buying good-quality roses.

The following are some of the problems likely to be encountered in the garden.

APHIDS
How to identify: The aphid that most commonly attacks roses is greenfly, usually spotted near the start of the growing season on the tips of stems and on developing flower buds.
Control: Spray the plants with a proprietary systemic insecticide as soon as an infestation is noticed,

ABOVE: *It is almost inevitable that aphids such as greenfly or blackfly will attack at some point during the season. The best control is vigilance and quick action with an appropriate insecticide.*

and repeat as directed by the manufacturer. Some insecticides are selective in their action and leave beneficial insects such as ladybirds unharmed.

Alternatively, spray with a solution of washing-up liquid or even with plain water, to disperse the pest, though such treatments will have to be repeated daily.

Though infestations are sometimes heavy, the pest is easy to control and long-term damage can be avoided.

BALLING
How to identify: Petals turn brown and cling together so that the flower fails to open. Most likely in wet weather.
Control: None possible. Balling is a seasonal problem that does not affect the overall health of the plant, but it is worth removing balled flowers. Apart from their unsightly appear-

ance, they are prone to rot, which may allow other diseases to take hold. Roses with very delicate petals are particularly susceptible.

BLACKSPOT
How to identify: Black spots or patches develop on the leaves and, in some cases, the stems, from mid-summer onwards. The leaves yellow and eventually drop off. Plants left untreated may eventually die back.
Control: Remove all infected leaves and stems and destroy them, then spray the plant with an appropriate fungicide. If you need to cut the plant hard back, feed and water well to encourage a quick recovery. Blackspot is more common in certain geographical areas and some rose varieties are more susceptible than others. Where blackspot is known to be a problem, spray with a fungicide as a precaution. In severe cases, replace the plants with disease-resistant varieties.

ABOVE: *Balling is caused by wet weather. It is not a common problem but some varieties are prone to it.*

mildew

rust

blackspot

LEFT: *Symptoms of the three most serious rose diseases.*

PROLIFERATION

How to identify: An unusual condition in which the stem continues to grow through the open flower, producing a further bud or cluster of buds. It is usually caused by damage to the stem while it is growing, perhaps by frost or a virus.

Control: Cut off affected stems. If only one or a few stems are affected, further steps are unnecessary, but where the whole plant has the condition a virus is probably the culprit and the whole plant should be dug up and destroyed.

ABOVE: *Proliferation is an unusual physiological disorder, perhaps caused by injury to the growing tip. In most cases, cutting out the affected stem is all that is necessary.*

MILDEW

How to identify: A whitish-grey powdering on the leaves and stems, which if not treated may cover the whole plant.

Control: Spray with a proprietary fungicide. Thin out congested growth. Where the overall planting is thick, and air circulation is therefore poor, replant to ensure more space around the plants.

RUST

How to identify: Orange spots that turn to black appear on the undersides of leaves from mid-summer onwards. If left untreated, rose rust can be fatal to the plant.

Control: Remove infected parts then spray with an appropriate fungicide (some fungicides are not very effective against rose rust). Thin out growth and improve air circulation around the plants as for mildew.

DIEBACK

How to identify: Flower buds, where present, fail to mature and wither. Beginning at the tip of the stem, leaves begin to wither and drop off. The stem itself droops and may blacken.

Control: Cut back all affected growth to healthy wood, then feed the plant well during the growing season to encourage new growth.

REPLANT DISEASE

How to identify: The roses suddenly fail to thrive and begin to die back. It usually occurs where roses have been grown in the same soil for many years.

Control: Dig up and discard the affected roses, then replace the top 30 cm (12 in) of the soil with fresh topsoil. Replant with fresh stock.

PRUNING: HYBRID TEAS

Hybrid tea (large-flowered) roses usually have large, fully double flowers with a high pointed centre, though as new varieties are developed the distinction between these and some floribundas (cluster-flowered roses) is becoming less clear than it used to be. A good rose catalogue will tell you whether your rose is a hybrid tea variety, but it is not serious if you get it wrong. Even if a hybrid tea is pruned as a floribunda there will still be a pleasing display of flowers.

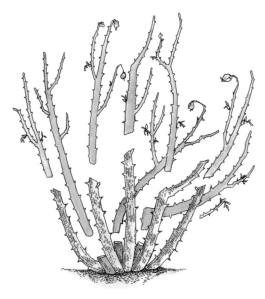

ABOVE: *To make the pruning easier, start by cutting out any badly positioned, diseased or dead wood (shown here coloured brown) close to the base. This will leave fewer stems about which pruning decisions have to be made, and the extra space makes the job easier. Shorten the remaining stems by about half, cutting to an outward-facing bud whenever possible.*

1 Hybrid tea roses look very different depending on whether or not they have been pruned regularly. This rose has been pruned annually and is not particularly congested. If you have a rose that has not been pruned for many years, there will be more dead wood and crossing shoots to be removed, but otherwise pruning is exactly the same. Start by cutting out dead or diseased shoots. This will make it easier to see what remains to be done.

3 *(Right)* Prune all the main stems by about half, or to within 20–25 cm (8–10 in) of the ground. The exact amount you cut off is not critical and is a matter of personal experience and choice. Try to bear in mind the final shape of the bush. Wherever possible, prune to an outward-pointing bud to give the bush more spread rather than a congested centre.

2 Remove badly placed, crossing or very congested shoots. Most of these can be cut back to their point of origin, but if growth is sparse cut to just above a healthy bud, close to the base. Prune out or shorten any very thin, spindly shoots. If there are plenty of other shoots, cut back to the point of origin. If there are few shoots, you may prefer to cut back to about two or three buds from the base of the shoot.

4 *(Above)* This is what the bush will probably look like after pruning. Although it is sparse at this stage, vigorous new growth will soon transform its appearance.

5 *(Right)* This is what can be expected a few months later if a hybrid tea rose has been pruned properly: even healthy growth and plenty of perfect flowers.

You Can Be Rough!

If you have a lot of roses to prune, simply going over the rose bed with a powered hedge-trimmer (shears) may be an appealing option. To traditionalists this sounds horrifying, but trials of the "rough and ready" method have shown that floribundas and hybrid teas can actually produce a better display than when pruned conventionally. However, there could be drawbacks: the bushes may become too congested, diseases may become a problem due to the more congested growth and because the dead wood on each plant is not being monitored individually.

For a general garden display, however, this method is well worth considering, especially if you keep an eye open for dead or diseased shoots to prune out at the same time.

Although a powered hedge-trimmer will save time, you can use secateurs for the same kind of effect, just topping the shoots at the required level.

RIGHT: *As part of a trial these roses were pruned with a hedge-trimmer. Despite this crude treatment, they performed just as well the following summer as roses pruned in the traditional way.*

PRUNING: FLORIBUNDAS

Floribunda roses, sometimes called cluster-flowered roses, have many flowers open at once in the same cluster, and are noted for their prolific blooming. Although most varieties have flattish flowers with relatively few petals, some have almost hybrid tea-shaped blooms with lots of petals and more pointed flowers. If in doubt, a good rose catalogue will tell you whether a particular variety is a floribunda – though no great harm will befall your rose if you get it wrong.

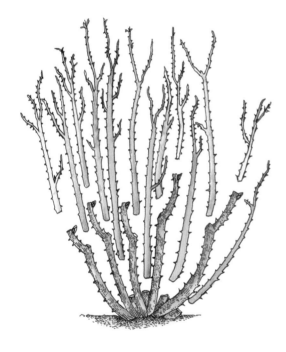

ABOVE: First cut out any badly placed or very old shoots that are dying or diseased (shown coloured brown), then shorten the remaining main shoots to about 45 cm (18 in), or about half their length. Cut back to an outward-facing bud where possible.

1 Floribunda roses often look more "twiggy" than hybrid teas, regardless of how they were pruned the previous year. Do not be deterred if they appear to have a confusing tangle of thorny shoots. After removing unhealthy shoots just start pruning from one side and work across each plant.

2 Start by cutting out dead or diseased shoots (ignore dieback at the tips of shoots at this stage, as they will probably be removed with the rest of the stem later). Cut these unwanted shoots back to their point of origin if there are plenty of other stems, otherwise to a point just above a healthy bud close to the base.

3 Next, remove any crossing or very badly placed branches. Cut out completely if necessary, or back to a bud pointing in a better direction. Also remove any very thin, spindly shoots coming from near the base of the bush.

4 Cut all the main stems back to about 45 cm (18 in), but use some discretion to reflect the size and vigour of the variety.

5 There will probably be some long sideshoots remaining on the main stems. Shorten these by cutting off between one-third and two-thirds of their length. Cut back to a bud pointing outwards rather than towards the centre of the bush.

6 This is what the bushes will probably look like after pruning. The framework is already well established, and new growth will soon restore the plants to their summer height.

7 A well-pruned floribunda rose will produce plenty of new, vigorous, even growth and an abundance of flowers.

Spread the Flowering

Although the bushes will look less even in growth, it is possible to extend the flowering season a little by leaving some shoots unpruned. These should flower earlier, followed by the pruned shoots. If this method is adopted, be sure to cut back the unpruned shoots the following year. Do not leave any shoots unpruned for more than two years.

When to Prune

For hybrid tea and floribunda roses, autumn and spring pruning both have their advocates. A good compromise is to shorten the height of very tall varieties by about half in the autumn, to reduce wind resistance that would cause wind-rock damage by loosening the roots. This is unnecessary with compact varieties. Most people prefer to prune their roses in early spring when new growth is beginning but before the leaves start to expand.

PRUNING: SHRUB ROSES

In pruning terms, shrub roses include any species of wild rose and old-fashioned varieties of bushy roses that pre-date hybrid teas and floribundas. Modern shrub roses, raised in recent times but retaining many of the characteristics of the traditional old-fashioned types, are pruned in the same way.

They generally make much bigger bushes than hybrid tea and floribunda types, but do not require such regular or intensive pruning. The main objective of annual pruning is to prevent the bushes becoming too large or congested.

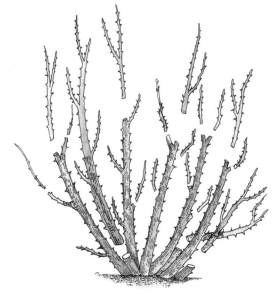

ABOVE: *Pruning should always be modified to suit the growth characteristics of the plant but, as a guide, shorten the main stems by between a quarter and a half, and any sideshoots that remain by about two-thirds. Cut out any badly positioned or diseased stems completely.*

1 Most species and early shrub roses will continue to flower well even without pruning, but become large and congested. Pruning will improve the overall appearance and help to keep the shrub compact.

2 After some years there will be a lot of very old wood, and probably congested stems. On an old plant, cut out one or two of the oldest or most congested shoots, taking them back to the base. Cut out any dead or diseased wood at the same time.

The rose illustrated naturally produces a lot of cane-like stems from the base; others will have fewer but thicker stems, more like those on a hybrid tea.

3 Shorten the main shoots (those that arise from the base of the plant, not sideshoots) by between a quarter and a half. If the shoot is 1.2 m (4 ft) tall, cut off 30–60 cm (1–2 ft).

If the shrub has also produced a lot of sideshoots (those growing off the main stems), shorten these by about two-thirds. If the sideshoot is 30 cm (12 in) long, cut back to about 10 cm (4 in).

4 Even when pruning has been done, you may be left with a substantial framework of stems. This is normal, as a shrub rose usually makes a large bush. With those that shoot freely from the base, like this one, you can be more drastic.

5 *(Left)* Annual pruning will ensure there is plenty of vigorous young growth from the base of the plant, keeping the size compact and ensuring plenty of flowers even close to the ground.

PRUNING: CLIMBERS

Climbing roses can seem daunting to prune. Not only is there physically a lot of growth to deal with, there are also different techniques to use according to the flowering habit of the variety. First decide whether the variety to be pruned is a repeat-flowerer, then follow the appropriate technique described.

ONCE-FLOWERING CLIMBERS

These have a permanent framework of woody stems, usually with very few new shoots growing from the base. They are best pruned in summer, when flowering has finished.

ABOVE: *On a well-established once-flowering climber, cut out one or two of the oldest stems to a point just above a new shoot close to the base. If there are no suitable low-growing new shoots, choose a point higher up the plant where there is one. Dead-head all the remaining shoots.*

1 Because these climbers have a stable framework of woody shoots, and are pruned in full leaf after flowering, they can often be intimidating to prune. Fortunately they usually flower well with minimal pruning, provided the plant is kept free of dead and diseased wood.

ABOVE: *A climbing rose in full bloom.*

2 Try to cut out one or two of the oldest stems (this will not be necessary on plants only a few years old), to increase the amount of new growth. If you can find a young replacement shoot near the base, cut to just above this. If there are no low-growing new shoots, choose a replacement perhaps 30–60 cm (1–2 ft) up the stem. Tie in the new growth to replace the shoot you have just removed.

Do not remove more than one-third of the stems, otherwise flowering will suffer the next year.

3 Go along the remaining stems and shorten the sideshoots to leave two or three buds.

REPEAT-FLOWERING CLIMBERS

These generally bloom from mid-summer through to autumn, although after the first flush the flowers may be fewer and more sporadic. The terms "perpetual-flowering" or "remontant" may also be used to describe these roses. They flower on new wood, but as relatively few new main shoots are produced, little pruning is required.

BELOW: A climbing rose trained up a tripod lends height to a border. Trim back any shoots that are growing too tall for the support.

1 During the summer, dead-head as the flowers fade, unless the plant is too large for this to be practical. Cut back to the nearest leaf.

2 In early spring, just shorten the shoots that flowered the previous summer, if the plant is growing too tall. Drastic pruning or reshaping should not be necessary unless the rose has been neglected. After shortening the tips of the main shoots, go along each stem in turn to identify which sideshoots flowered in the summer and cut them back to two or three buds.

3 Remove entirely any shoots that are badly positioned, and cut out any dead or diseased wood. The basic outline of the rose may not look very different after pruning, but it will ensure that there are plenty of flowers in future years.

PRUNING: RAMBLERS

Rambler roses produce new stems freely from the base, rather than growing steadily taller on old stems. This gives them a lower, more spreading growth habit. They flower once – in mid- or late summer – and usually have large trusses of small blooms. As they flower on shoots produced the previous year, pruning is best done when flowering is over.

1 Prune after flowering – late summer is a good time. Old, congested plants can be more daunting than young ones, but they will not present a problem if the pruning is done methodically.

2 First cut out any dead or damaged shoots, or those that are very weak and spindly. Do not remove vigorous young shoots.

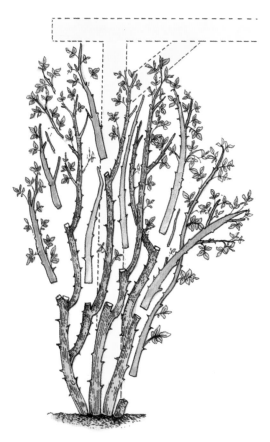

ABOVE: *Ramblers are straightforward to prune. Cut back old canes that have flowered, taking them back to a point where there is a new replacement shoot. Do not prune out an old shoot unless there is a new one to replace it, but remove completely any very old, dead or diseased wood.*

3 Cut out old spent canes that have flowered, but only where there are new shoots to replace them. Once you have a well-established rambler, try to balance the shoots that you remove with those available to replace them. This will vary from plant to plant and year to year. On any old flowered canes that have been retained, shorten the sideshoots to leave two or three leaves.

4 Tie in new shoots to the support. Wherever possible, tie loosely to horizontal wires or a trellis.

5 (Opposite) Rambler roses like this will flower prolifically every summer. Regular pruning ensures that old wood is replaced by vigorous new growth so that the plant is clothed with flowers from top to bottom.

Pillar Roses

Pillar roses are similar to ramblers but are grown in a column shape up a post or pillar. Growth is usually upright and the rather rigid stems are seldom much more than 2.4 m (8 ft) tall. They are repeat-flowering and bloom on the current season's wood. Good rose catalogues indicate which varieties are most suitable for growing in this way.

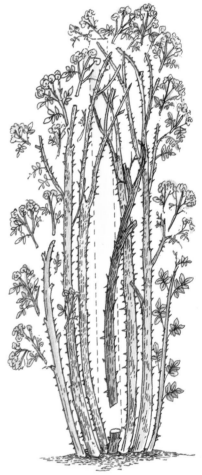

Pillar roses require regular pruning only once they are well established. Apart from cutting out one or two of the oldest stems each year, the only pruning required is to shorten shoots that have flowered to maintain an attractive shape. This is best done in late summer to early winter.

PRUNING: STANDARDS

The pruning of standard roses can appear confusing, and even gardeners very confident about pruning bush roses sometimes feel uneasy about this task. However, if the pruning is directed to forming an attractive, rounded head, there are few difficulties.

Weeping standards are dealt with differently. These are pruned in summer – after flowering – and not in spring like a normal standard.

PRUNING A NORMAL STANDARD

1 (Right) Do not be deterred by the apparent tangle of shoots, just keep a rounded head in mind as you work through the pruning methodically.

BELOW: If it is well pruned in the dormant season, a standard rose will produce a rounded head of even growth that makes a ball of beautiful blooms.

ABOVE: Prune an ordinary standard rose (left) by shortening the summer's growth by about half. Prune a weeping standard (right) by cutting back each long shoot to a point where there is a new one to replace it. If no suitable replacement shoots can be found, do not prune the main stems; instead, shorten the sideshoots on the flowered stems to two buds.

2 During late winter or early spring, shorten the main stems in the head to about six buds, more or less depending on the age of the plant.

Do not prune too hard, as this may stimulate over-vigorous shoots that could spoil the shape. Cut to an outward-facing bud, to encourage a good shape.

5 *(Right)* Aim to leave a rounded head of reasonably evenly spaced branches. Although the rose looks unattractive at this stage, try to visualize it with the new shoots growing from this framework.

3 Old plants may have areas of dead or diseased wood. Cut affected shoots back to healthy buds.

4 Shorten sideshoots growing from the main stem to a couple of buds, to stop growth becoming too congested.

Pruning a Weeping Standard

Weeping standards, which sometimes have their shoots trained over an umbrella-shaped frame, are really rambling roses grafted on to a single stem. For this reason they are pruned like ramblers in summer or early autumn, when flowering has finished, and not in the dormant season.

If pruning is not done annually growth can become congested and tangled.

While pruning, take the opportunity to check that the stake is sound, and that ties are not too tight.

It takes a few years to produce a weeping rose as well clothed with flowering shoots as this. Once a good head has been achieved, maintain it by cutting some of the oldest shoots back to a point where there is a young replacement.

PROPAGATION

Propagating roses is satisfying and fun, and even if they are not needed for your own garden they make ideal gifts for friends.

Commercially, roses are budded on to rootstocks, but this is an impractical technique for amateurs, for whom rootstocks can be difficult to obtain. Fortunately, perfectly satisfactory roses can be grown from cuttings.

The bushes of some kinds, such as hybrid teas, may be less vigorous than those budded on to a rootstock, but climbers, ramblers and most shrub roses do very well on their own roots, and because there is no rootstock you will not have to worry about suckers.

Semi-ripe cuttings are taken in mid- or late summer, hardwood cuttings in autumn or early winter. Most gardeners find taking hardwood cuttings easier because this method does not require any special equipment and aftercare is minimal.

HARDWOOD CUTTINGS

Prepare a trench about 23–30 cm (9–12 in) deep in the open ground and line it to one-third of its depth with sharp sand.

Cut well-ripened, pencil-thick stems from the rose, remove the soft tip of each and trim to a length of about 23 cm (9 in), making the basal cut just below a leaf joint. Remove any leaves that remain on the stem. Dip the base of each cutting in a rooting hormone, then place it in the trench, leaving about 7.5 cm (3 in) above the surface. Firm the cuttings in and water well.

If hard frosts cause soil erosion, it may be necessary to refirm the cuttings during the winter. Keep them well watered in dry weather and remove any flower buds that form during the growing season.

The cuttings should be rooted by the autumn following planting. If they are sufficiently developed they can be transferred to their final position in the garden; otherwise allow them to grow on for another year.

SEMI-RIPE CUTTINGS

1 Select a sideshoot that is still green but beginning to turn woody at the base. Cut just above an outward-facing bud.

2 Trim the cutting at the base, just below a leaf joint.

3 Trim back the soft tip to leave a stem about 10 cm (4 in) long.

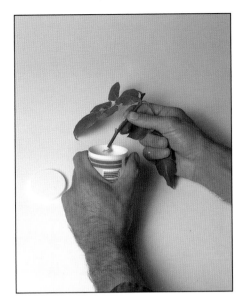

4 Remove the lower leaves and any thorns. Dip the base of the cutting in a rooting hormone powder, and tap off the excess.

5 Fill a pot with a mixture of two parts sharp sand to one part peat. Use a small dibber to make holes, and insert the cuttings up to two-thirds of their length in the rooting medium.

6 Firm the cuttings into the soil with your fingers, then spray them gently with a copper fungicide to moisten the compost and kill off any fungal spores.

7 *(Left)* Label the cuttings, then enclose the pot in a clear plastic bag to prevent moisture loss. Support the bag with cane or wire hoops to prevent contact between the plastic and the leaves, as moisture from the condensation may cause the leaves to rot. Keep the cuttings in a shady, frost-free place until rooted.

ABOVE: *After about six to eight weeks, roots will start to form, as shown here, and the cuttings will begin to grow. The plants can slowly be hardened off, but do not be in too much of a hurry to pot them up individually. Wait until the roots are well formed.*

$\mathscr{A}$ YEAR IN THE ROSE GARDEN

$\mathscr{E}$ARLY SPRING

ABOVE: *Prune hybrid teas and floribundas once the winter frosts are over and as soon as new growth begins.*

- Improve the soil and plant new stock.
- Finish spring pruning before the new leaves emerge if possible.
- On all types of rose, cut out any dead, diseased or damaged wood.
- Hoe in a rose fertilizer around the bases of the plants as growth emerges, then water in well. If the ground has been mulched, draw back the mulch before applying the fertilizer.
- Mulch or top up an existing mulch.
- Renovate neglected plants by pruning and feeding.

$\mathscr{M}$ID- AND LATE SPRING

ABOVE: *Dig a generously sized hole in well-prepared soil when planting a container rose.*

- Check for signs of aphids such as greenfly, and begin pest control.
- Continue to plant new roses.

$\mathscr{E}$ARLY SUMMER

ABOVE: *Rotted manure makes an effective mulch and also adds nutrients to the soil.*

- Control weeds.
- Mulch if you have not already done so, but choose a day when the ground is moist.
- Spray as necessary to control pests and diseases.

$\mathscr{M}$ID-SUMMER

ABOVE: *Try to find the time to remove individual spent flowers to keep roses looking their best.*

- Dead-head regularly except for varieties which have decorative hips.
- Feed with a rose fertilizer (or a general-purpose balanced fertilizer if you prefer).
- Increase your stock by taking semi-ripe cuttings.
- Check for, and control, blackspot, rust and mildew.
- Plant new container-grown stock.
- Trim rose hedges after flowering, unless they will have decorative hips.
- Prune ramblers and weeping standards when they have finished flowering.

LATE SUMMER

ABOVE: *Once you have pruned out old stems of ramblers and climbers, tie in vigorous new shoots to replace them.*

• Tie in strong new shoots of climbers and ramblers to extend the framework.

• Continue to take semi-ripe cuttings.

• Send off rose orders for autumn planting.

AUTUMN

• Hoe in bonemeal around the base of the plants, and water in well.

• Order new plants.

• Prepare and plant new beds.

• Take hardwood cuttings.

• In a windy or very exposed garden, shorten long shoots of hybrid tea and floribunda roses to reduce winter wind-rock (complete the pruning in spring).

RIGHT: *Choose a spare piece of ground that is airy but lightly shaded in which to plant hardwood cuttings.*

WINTER

• Tidy up hedges with ornamental hips (such as *Rosa rugosa*) that were not pruned after flowering.

• Plant new roses, provided the ground is not frozen or waterlogged.

• Prepare the ground for roses to be planted in spring.

ABOVE: *Dig a large hole when planting a bush, shrub, or old-fashioned rose. Add bonemeal to the soil that will surround the plant to promote root growth.*

ROSES AROUND THE GARDEN

Roses are a favourite with every gardening enthusiast. Even a solitary rose makes a great focal point in any part of the garden. The following section is a practical look at different planting methods and combinations that will inspire you to ever-greater creativity.

ROSES AROUND THE GARDEN

Roses are often grown in dedicated beds or in areas of the garden devoted solely to them, but they are very versatile plants that can be used imaginatively all around the garden. The following pages show some of the interesting and beautiful ways in which roses can be used.

Some rose enthusiasts prefer to create a rose garden in which few other plants feature, but there is a risk that such a strategy will leave the garden looking bare and boring for a large part of the year. Others are put off planting more roses simply because of the short period of interest with some types, especially the once-flowering climbers and ramblers and some of the species and old-fashioned roses. By using roses imaginatively, however, it is possible to enjoy all their charm and beauty without sacrificing any of the delights of your garden.

PREVIOUS PAGE: Rosa 'Fantin Latour'.

ABOVE: *Use climbers and ramblers to clothe otherwise boring fences and walls: even when flowering is over, the foliage will act as a pleasing green screen for the rest of summer and into autumn. Here 'Madame Alfred Carrière', which continues to flower intermittently into the autumn, is doing a magnificent job enhancing a boundary.*

ABOVE: *Plant roses in mixed borders, just like any other desirable flowering shrub. Here the yellow floribunda 'Chinatown' looks perfectly in place.*

LEFT: *Roses can soften and disguise harsh structures like the garden shed. This is the fragrant and almost thornless 'Blush Rambler'.*

ABOVE: *Small trees can make excellent supports for climbers and ramblers. In this instance, the rambler 'Bobbie James' gives an apple tree a second flush of blossom.*

Purists may prefer their roses unadulterated, but most gardeners appreciate other plants too and one plant can often be used to enhance another. A rambling rose such as 'Wedding Day' climbing through a flowering cherry will drape the branches with creamy white flowers a month or two after the cherry blossom is over – giving two displays instead of one. A late-flowering clematis growing though a climbing or rambling rose will double the flowering capacity of a given space. Anyone with a strong sense of colour co-ordination might like to plant a clematis that flowers at the same time as the rose, creating an even more stunning effect. Prune the clematis back hard in early spring.

Roses can be used along with other shrubs in shrub or mixed borders, or used as hedges, flowering ground cover, or even as container plants. In recent years, breeders have created more versatile varieties with a much wider range of uses as well as longer flowering periods, opening up many possibilities for using them all around the garden.

ABOVE: *The clever positioning of a rose with an ornament or urn can lend structure to the planting and give a pleasing contrast of form. This is 'Golden Celebrations', a modern shrub.*

ABOVE: *Shrub roses look perfectly in place in a shrub or mixed border, and ramblers, climbers or pillar roses can be grown up supports to give height to the border.*

LEFT: *Roses can make charming container plants, but they must have an adequate volume of soil, and regular watering in dry weather is essential.*

HAPPY MARRIAGES

For some stunning effects, try interplanting your roses with other plants that make happy combinations of colour and form. Purists may consider this detracts from the roses, but as a garden feature roses can be enhanced by what you plant with them.

Pansies provide a simple solution if you just want to cover the ground between the roses, especially in winter and spring when the roses are not in leaf. In summer they will find it difficult to compete in the shade except at the edge of the border. Polyanthus are also useful for spring colour.

In summer, when the roses are in bloom, their companions need to be stronger and bolder plants. Annual grasses are easily planted among existing roses, but choose a variety of grass that does not grow taller than the rose. Lavenders and catmints (nepetas), with their blue, lavender or purple flowers, are popular companions, but these are permanent features in the bed and the spacing of the roses should allow for both plants.

ABOVE: *Lavenders and roses make pleasing companions, and offer a double dose of fragrance. This is* Lavandula angustifolia *acting as a pleasing backdrop for a pink rose.*

ABOVE: *Shrub roses and even ramblers are ideal for mixed borders if they can be given space to grow to their full potential. In this mainly white border, the white ramblers 'Félicité et Perpétue', 'Bobbie James' and 'Adélaïde d'Orléans' blend in beautifully among the other plants.*

It is worth experimenting with the unlikely, such as yellow day lilies (hemerocallis) with yellow roses or pink gypsophila interplanted among pink roses.

Always bear in mind that for tip-top roses you will need to feed, spray and, with some roses, regularly dead-head, so plants that make rose cultivation difficult may mean a sacrifice of quality of bloom.

RIGHT: Blues and reds or blues and pinks look good together, and the small flowers of catmints (nepetas) create a wash of background colour without competing with the roses.

BELOW: Feathery ornamental grasses make striking companions, softening the stiff starkness of the rose stems and bringing a sense of movement as they sway in the wind.

ABOVE: Clematis make ideal partners for roses, and here one acts as a bridge between 'Madame Alfred Carrière' and 'Bobbie James'. Clematis can be chosen to flower at the same time or to extend the period of interest by blooming later. If the clematis is to grow through the rose itself, where its stems will become entwined, selecting a late-flowering variety that needs cutting back hard in early spring will make the task of pruning more practicable.

$\mathscr{B}$EAUTIFUL BEDS

Many roses, especially hybrid teas and floribundas, look best when massed in a rose bed. Where space is unrestricted, whole beds of a single variety can look stunning, especially when fragrance matches the perfection of bloom. Beds of mixed roses can also be very pleasing, but for impact plant in groups of about five plants of each variety and select varieties that harmonize well in terms of size and habit as well as colour.

Rose beds are most appropriate in a formal rose garden, with rectangular or circular beds set into the lawn, ideally with pergolas or arches clothed with climbers and ramblers. This kind of garden is a rose-lover's paradise, especially if it is set with suitably positioned seats surrounded by fragrance. Many enthusiasts willingly forego other plants for such bliss and beauty.

Floribundas are ideal for beds designed to be viewed from a distance, where a mass of blooms over a long period is more important than the quality of individual flowers. Beds of hybrid tea roses generally have less impact from a distance, and flowering can be more uneven, especially where there are many varieties in the same bed. This is irrelevant for those rose lovers who prefer to savour the beauty of individual blooms.

Many modern gardens are too small for formal rose beds set in a large lawn, but there is plenty of

ABOVE: A formal rose garden is the ideal way to grow roses. Both visual impact and scent are concentrated, and it is a magical place to sit on a hot summer's day. Large rose beds like these have space for many different kinds of rose, but even in a small rose garden it is important to use pergolas or frames for climbers to provide the essential element of height.

scope for patio beds. Choose low-growing floribunda varieties (sometimes described as patio roses) for small beds set into the patio. Patio and miniature roses are also ideal for raised beds, where they can replace seasonal bedding plants. Although the initial investment is greater, the money you save on seasonal bedding will recover the cost of the roses over a few seasons.

TOP RIGHT: Part of the famous Royal National Rose Society garden at Chiswell Green, near St Albans, Hertfordshire. This is one of the finest rose gardens in England, where rose beds abound and you can assess a wide range of varieties in a garden setting.

RIGHT: Rose beds have more impact if they are densely planted. The pink rose in the foreground of this picture is 'The Fairy', a polyantha rose.

BORDER BEAUTIES

Roses are ideal border plants, whether in mixed plantings, or in a border dedicated to roses. Many varieties have a long flowering season that will out-perform most other flowering shrubs . . . and of course they contribute the special charm of their perfume.

If space rules out formal rose beds cut into the lawn, it is usually possible to create a rose border. Instead of filling it with herbaceous plants, pack it with roses of all kinds and colours. It will look spectacular in early and mid-summer, and will continue to offer pockets of interest right through until autumn.

Use shrub roses and pillar roses at the back of the border, modern shrub roses and the taller floribundas towards the centre, and compact floribundas and hybrid teas towards the front, with some of the long-flowering ground cover roses as an edging. A kaleidoscope of colour works best with this kind of rose border, and enables many varieties to be grown.

Rose borders are ideal for old-fashioned and modern shrub roses, many of which are too tall or bushy for formal rose beds. These roses also have a more informal shape more appropriate for a shrub border.

Use shrub roses to transform an existing shrub border that looks tired and boring, perhaps with large shrubs at the back that are mainly grown for their foliage. Shrub roses planted in front of large established shrubs will bring the border to life in summer, and the foliage behind makes a pleasing backdrop against which to view the roses. Species roses, especially the tall-growing kinds such as *Rosa moyesii*, grown for its decorative hips, and *R. sericea omeiensis pteracantha*, grown mainly for its spectacular thorns, are also ideal in this situation.

If there is no space for a formal rose garden or a rose border, integrate as many roses as possible into a mixed border. If you can make the border a viewpoint from an arbour of roses, or a sitting area framed by roses, so much the better.

ABOVE: *Use ramblers, climbers and other tall roses at the back of a rose border. This takes the eye right to the back of the border and the extra height ensures the feature is a focal point even from a distance.*

LEFT: *A plain dark green hedge makes a good background against which to view a rose border. Pale colours like this 'Dapple Dawn', a shrub rose, show up particularly well.*

BELOW: *Try to incorporate a sitting area where you can linger to admire your rose border. Frame it with fragrant roses, perhaps using climbing roses to create a sense of enclosure like this. Use roses as a unifying theme to link different parts of the garden.*

OLD-FASHIONED CHARM

The *grandes dames* of the summer border, unsurpassed for their sumptuous flowers and heady fragrance, old roses still have a place in every garden. That they have endured so long is thanks not only to their beauty but also in many cases to their ease of cultivation.

Old roses lend themselves to an informal, mixed, cottage style of planting that also uses other shrubs, hardy perennials and summer bulbs. Many make large, spreading plants that need some form of support, though you can allow them to flop gracefully over and through

neighbouring shrubs. Some gallicas, Chinas and tea roses, however, grow no larger than 1.2 m (4 ft), which makes them suitable for the smallest garden. The English roses raised by David Austin have flowers with the appearance of old roses even though they are of modern origin, but they are generally compact shrubs that fit well in a small garden.

Try to create traditional cottage-garden groupings with old roses in mixed borders. The geometric shapes of alliums such as *A. sphaerocephalon* and *A. giganteum* are the perfect foil to the lax habit of many shrub roses, as are the strong verticals of foxgloves (*Digitalis purpurea*). The white or apricot-pink forms of the digitalis, or the milky blue or white Canterbury bell (*Campanula medium*), are particularly effective, and both are biennials easily raised from seed. The perennial *Campanula lactiflora* also works well.

For a less spiky, more integrated effect, use easy border perennials such as hardy geraniums, lady's mantle (*Alchemilla mollis*) or catmint (*Nepeta* x *faassenii*), all of which blend with most other plants. Clouds of perennial gypsophila (*G. paniculata*) or bronze fennel (*Foeniculum vulgare* 'Purpureum') will further soften the edges.

LEFT: *Lavender and lady's mantle (*Alchemilla mollis*) are perfect partners for old-fashioned roses and shrub roses of all kinds.*

Grey-leaved plants always look good with the soft pinks and crimsons of old roses. Try *Artemisia lactiflora*, lamb's ears (*Stachys byzantina*), and *Senecio* (now more correctly *Brachyglottis*) 'Sunshine'. The latter has yellow daisy flowers in summer, but you can remove these to prevent them clashing with the roses.

Underplant tall roses with something to clothe the ground, such as hostas, lavender, or the grey-leaved curry plant (*Helichrysum italicum*). The last two will only do well in a sunny position, however, whereas the hostas tolerate shade.

A SCENTED BORDER

Roses are indispensable for a scented border. To create a pot-pourri of scents, provide a backdrop of mock orange (philadelphus), the flowering of which will coincide with the roses' main mid-summer flush. Underplant with old-fashioned pinks such as the clove-scented 'Gran's Favourite', and try to include the heady fragrance of *Lilium regale* or the incense-scented ornamental tobacco *Nicotiana alata*.

ABOVE: Old roses like this gallica 'Duc de Guiche', known since 1835, are perfect for shrub and rose borders in the modern garden.

ABOVE: Rosa moyesii is an invaluable species rose to grow among old-fashioned roses in the border. In summer its attractive single red flowers (left) are a feature, while autumn brings a bonus of stems festooned with flagon-shaped hips (right).

LEFT: Including some species roses with decorative hips will prolong the period of interest. Rosa pimpinellifolia, sometimes catalogued under its older name of R. spinosissima, is the Scotch or Burnet rose, with cream, white or pink flowers and very dark hips that eventually become almost black.

HEDGES AND BOUNDARIES

arden walls and fences are essentially functional: they are there to define the boundaries, to keep children and pets in and intruders out. For a rose lover they are also a wonderful opportunity to plant more roses.

Walls and fences represent golden opportunities for planting climbing and rambling roses. Climbers can be planted against tall walls, while ramblers are a better choice for lower walls and fences. However, even tall climbers and ramblers will spread horizontally along a fence if they cannot grow upwards.

Fix horizontal supports about 45–60 cm (1½–2 ft) apart, and train as many shoots as possible along these. New shoots will grow from this framework of horizontal branches to cover most of the wall or fence, whereas if all the shoots are allowed to grow upwards most of the flowers will be bunched together at the top and then simply tumble down over each other.

A Thorny Question

Rose hedges must not become neglected, especially those that border a public footpath. Overgrown roses with thorny shoots that catch on passers-by soon lead to disputes. If necessary, plant a little further into the garden and not right at the edge, so that they do not overhang the path.

ABOVE: 'Albertine', one of the all-time favourites among ramblers, looks wonderful growing against a tall boundary wall. It flowers prolifically and fills the air with scent. Only a susceptibility to mildew mars this choice: this will be less of a problem if it is grown over an openwork fence.

BELOW: Brick walls make an ideal background against which to view climbing roses, and in return the flowers soften the harshness of too much brickwork.

ABOVE: A living wall of roses can make a delightful garden boundary. Even grown over quite a flimsy frame of trelliswork or chain link, roses soon provide dense cover that gives a sense of privacy in summer.

RIGHT: A covering of roses can make even the oldest of fences look attractive and act as a further barrier.

A ROSE HEDGE

Roses can make beautiful boundaries, and are ideal for an internal dividing hedge within the garden, but they will not provide the sense of privacy that, say, a privet or yew hedge can impart. Although thorny stems will deter intruders and some animals, a rose hedge is best regarded as an ornamental feature. It will be informal in profile, and should not be clipped to a neat outline with shears.

Given these limitations, roses can make some of the best flowering hedging, blooming for far longer than most shrubs – sometimes with the bonus of scent. Few other hedges can match the rose for colour, length of flowering period, and fragrance.

Traditional choices are *Rosa rugosa* and its varieties such as 'Scabrosa', or the hybrid musks 'Cornelia' and 'Penelope'. All these will make a hedge 1.2 m (4 ft) or more tall. For a lower hedge try 'Ballerina', a lower-growing hybrid musk with white flowers flushed pink. The hydrangea-like clusters of musk-scented flowers bloom over a long period.

Tall floribunda roses also make pretty hedges, though they are less substantial than the shrub roses already mentioned. For that reason it is best to plant them in a double staggered row. Pleasing varieties for this purpose are 'Eye Paint' (red with a white centre), 'Margaret Merril' (white), 'Masquerade' (multicoloured) and 'Southampton' (apricot-orange).

LEFT: Part of a rose hedge using 'Hansa', one of the rugosa hybrids.

CARPETS OF COLOUR

Roses sound unpromising as ground cover plants, but there are varieties able to create a carpet of colour that will look beautiful all summer long. They could transform an area of neglected ground or perhaps a steep bank that is difficult to cultivate.

Some of the older ground cover roses can be disappointing: they can be too tall for a small area and their flowering season is sometimes short. These criticisms cannot be levelled against many of the compact ground cover roses bred in recent years: they literally form a carpet of bloom.

Roses will not form an impenetrable barrier against weeds like some of the more traditional evergreen ground cover shrubs, but weeds are least active while the roses are dormant and devoid of foliage,

so they can be quite effective weed suppressers if the ground is cleared of weeds first and then mulched. The best way to be sure of eliminating weeds is to plant the roses through a mulching sheet.

The term "ground cover rose" is used to describe varieties with very different habits: some are ground-hugging while others are relatively tall and arching. Some have a spread of about 60 cm (2 ft) while others may reach 3 m (10 ft) or more across. If you are considering a ground cover rose, always make certain that its size and growth habit are what you want. All have their place in the garden, but the right kind must be chosen for each situation.

These are the broad groups into which most ground cover roses fit, though a few fall between these broad brushstroke headings:

Tall ground cover roses with **arching stems** include 'Pink Bells' and 'Red Bells', which grow little more than 1 m (3 ft) tall but have a spread of about 1.2 m (4 ft) or more. The plants are smothered in double flowers in mid- and late summer. Prune them like shrub roses, but concentrate on shortening any branches which want to grow vertically.

ABOVE: 'Pink Bells', one of the larger ground cover roses, reaches about 1.2 m (4 ft), but it is a real eye-catcher where there is space for it.

ABOVE: 'Suffolk' is one of the brightest ground cover roses. It grows about 45 cm (1½ ft) tall and has a spread of about 1 m (3 ft).

LEFT: 'Essex' has spreading shoots that make a plant about 1.2 m (4 ft) wide.

Tall ground cover roses that are about as wide as they are tall include 'Rosy Cushion' (pink, single), 'Smarty' (rose-madder, single), 'Surrey' (pink, double, very long-flowering), and 'Sussex' (apricot-buff, double, with a long flowering season). Prune them like those with arching stems.

Ground-hugging varieties which spread wider than their height and usually creep along the ground include 'Flower Carpet' (bright pink, double, blooming over a very long period), 'Grouse' (pale pink, single flowers in mid- and late summer; less than 30 cm (1 ft) tall, but spreads to about 3 m (10 ft) across), 'Kent' (white, semi-double), 'Max Graf' (pink, single, grows to about 1.8 m (6ft) across), 'Nozomi' (white flushed pink, single), 'Pheasant' (pink, double, flowers in mid- and late summer, with a 3 m (10 ft) spread) and 'Snow Carpet' (white, double). All these require minimal pruning other than to shorten the longest stems to restrain their spread.

TOP RIGHT: 'Flower Carpet' is an outstanding variety with large, very bright blooms produced all summer and even into autumn.

MIDDLE RIGHT: A traditional ground cover rose, 'Grouse' lacks the brightness of many newer varieties but is useful for clothing a bank.

RIGHT: 'Nozomi' is sometimes classified as a climbing miniature, but unsupported it forms a ground cover shrub about 1.2 m (4 ft) across.

PLANTING GROUND COVER ROSES

Although ground cover roses will help to suppress weeds once they are well established, for real maintenance-free beds they should be planted through a sheet mulch.

Sheet mulches will not add nutrients to the soil or improve its structure as many organic "loose" mulches do, so thorough ground preparation is essential. Always incorporate plenty of humus-forming material such as garden compost or well-rotted manure, and rake in a balanced fertilizer if preparing the ground in spring, or a controlled-release fertilizer or bonemeal for autumn or winter planting.

2 Make cross-shaped planting slits in the sheet with a knife or scissors. If the rose's root-ball is large it may be necessary to make the slits large enough to take a spade, but the flaps can still simply be folded back into place afterwards.

3 Roses in a small container can be planted with a trowel, but a spade may be needed for large ones. Provided the ground was well prepared before the sheet was laid, it should be easy to dig out the planting hole.

1 Always prepare the ground thoroughly before laying the mulching sheet. Make a slit around the edge of the bed with a spade, and push the sheet into this. Firm the soil around the edge to ensure the sheet is held taut over the bed.

4 If the roses are already planted, but not too large, the sheet can be applied by making large slits at the positions of the plants, then slipping it over them. Simply fold the flaps back around the stems – it will not matter if the join is not perfect as it can be covered with a decorative mulch.

5 Although most of the sheet mulch will be hidden as the plants grow, initially it will be very conspicuous. A layer of a decorative mulch such as chipped bark or gravel will make it much more acceptable.

6 *(Right)* An inexpensive plastic mulch can be used for newly planted ground cover roses with a view to removing it once the plants are well established. Its appearance can be improved by covering it with chipped bark – as only a thin layer is required to hide the sheet, this should be cheaper than using a thick layer of chipped bark on its own.

Which Material?

Black polythene (plastic) is inexpensive and widely available. It does not allow water to penetrate, so it is best used in narrow strips, perhaps on either side of a newly planted rose hedge.

Woven plastic mulches are more expensive, but they allow water to seep through while suppressing weeds by keeping out the light.

There are a few sheet mulches that are made from biodegradable materials such as wool waste. This is a good option if the sheet mulch is required only while the roses are becoming established.

RIGHT: *'Pink Bells' makes suitable ground cover in a large garden.*

CLIMBERS AND RAMBLERS

There are few more idyllic images than that of a country cottage in high summer, the garden gate arched over and the house walls wreathed with roses. Not everyone has that kind of setting, but climbers and ramblers can be just as beautiful in a small modern town garden, if planted with imagination.

A climbing or rambling rose will lend an air of maturity and timelessness even to the most modern home. Try planting one of the heavily scented varieties such as 'Albertine', 'New Dawn' or 'Zéphirine Drouhin' by the front door, perhaps trained against a trellis. 'Zéphirine Drouhin' is a particularly useful variety for this position because it has no thorns to catch on clothing.

Climbing roses have a number of other uses in the garden. Where there is space, you could allow a climber or rambler to grow with the minimum of pruning to produce a huge fountain of flowers. The rambling 'Albertine' grown in this way would make a magnificent spectacle.

Climbing roses are also suitable for growing against pillars and pergolas. Rustic poles are appropriate in cottage gardens, although brick pillars are more substantial and permanent supports.

Some varieties can also be trained along ropes slung between two supports to create a flowering bower at the back of a border. For this purpose, choose a medium-growing

Mask the Bare Bits

Climbing roses tend to become bare at the base in time, so mask this by underplanting with easy perennials such as catmint (nepeta), lamb's ears (*Stachys byzantina*), lady's mantle (*Alchemilla mollis*) or hostas.

ABOVE: *Roses scrambling over an archway are quintessential ingredients of a country garden, though you can achieve a similar effect in an enclosed town garden too. As well as bringing a delightful froth of blooms high above the path, the archway creates a simple screening effect that offers an illusion of space.*

variety with long flexible stems, such as 'Madame Grégoire Staechelin', that can be looped around the rope to make swags of flowers.

Pillars, pyramids or tripods placed towards the back of the border can be covered with shorter-growing varieties such as 'Golden Showers' or 'Handel', or one of the Bourbon roses such as 'Madame Isaac Pereire' or 'Louise Odier'.

Free-standing trellis panels can be used to train the roses to, and they look particularly pleasing if painted white or in a colour that enhances the variety you are growing.

Very vigorous climbers, some of which can reach 10 m (30 ft) or more with a suitable support, are best accommodated by planting them where they can grow into a tree. 'Seagull' and 'Wedding Day' are among the varieties suitable for this.

Rambling roses can be grown informally by allowing them to scramble through large shrubs such as lilacs that are dull after their show of flowers in late spring or early summer. You can also plant them where they will trail over a fence to make a "curtain" of flowers.

ABOVE: If you have a pretty window like this, make the most of it by framing it with a climbing rose.

ABOVE: Be bold: try colour-coordinating your fence and roses. This pastel pink fence perfectly matches the climbing rose behind.

ABOVE: Climbing versions of hybrid tea and floribunda roses are best grown against a trellis on a wall or pillar. This is 'Climbing Iceberg'.

LEFT: Conifers do not make ideal supports for vigorous climbing or rambling roses, as they tend to cling to the surface instead of growing through the branches, but 'Seagull' is happy scaling the heights here.

RIGHT: Wooden pyramids or tripods make a solid support for climbers planted at the back of a border. This variety is 'Louise Odier'.

PLANTING A WALL CLIMBER

Roses need special care when planted against a wall, where a "rain shadow" means the soil is often dry. A decorative trellis will improve air circulation and help to make a feature of the new rose while it is becoming established.

A large trellis makes an attractive support for small climbers, though it is also possible to support them by means of galvanized or plastic-covered wire stretched between vine eyes fixed to the wall.

To ensure adequate air circulation between the plant and the wall, mount the trellis on battens. This also makes it easier to remove the plant if you need to paint or repair the wall.

Whichever method of support is chosen, take trouble over planting the rose, and be prepared to water it regularly during the first season. Even after rain the soil close to a house wall can be dry.

2 Screw the battens to the wall.

3 Nail the trellis to the battens.

4 Fork over the planting area, working in plenty of organic matter – in this case, spent mushroom compost. If the area is paved it may be necessary to remove some of the paving first.

5 Dig the planting hole at least 30 cm (1 ft) from the wall, and twice the depth and width of the container or roots. Fork in more organic matter and a handful of bonemeal or balanced fertilizer.

1 Decide on the best position for the trellis on the wall, then drill holes at suitable intervals to take the battens. Tap in plastic wall plugs to take the screws.

6 *(Left)* Check the planting depth, and adjust if necessary by adding or removing soil until the level is as required.

7 Remove the rose from its pot and gently tease out a few roots from around the edge of the root-ball to encourage the rose to root into the surrounding soil more quickly.

8 Position the rose in the hole, angling the top growth towards the wall. If planting a bare-root rose, fan the roots out away from the wall, to ensure they receive adequate moisture. Backfill with soil.

9 Firm the soil with your foot to ensure the rose is firmly planted and there are no large air pockets in which the roots might dry out.

10 Cut back any dead or damaged growth, but leave longer, healthy stems unpruned. Also remove any faded flowers.

11 If they are long enough, fan out the stems and tie them loosely to the trellis.

12 Finally, water in thoroughly. If planting in spring, fork a little rose or general balanced fertilizer around the base of the plant, at the rate recommended by the manufacturer. The rose should establish quickly and soon produce vigorous shoots that can be trained to the trellis.

RAISING STANDARDS

Standard roses lend height to rose beds and act as focal points, but they can be used just as effectively in summer bedding schemes and as container plants on the patio.

Roses grown as standards inevitably become focal points in a way that an individual bush rose seldom can. Not only are they raised above most of the other roses, they have an "architectural" shape that simply demands attention. For that reason a single specimen in the centre of a formal flower bed is often the centre of attention, and when planted in a rose bed a single plant can compete with perhaps dozens of lower-growing hybrid teas or floribundas in visual terms.

Be cautious when planting standards among other roses. Standards come in different heights (see box) and the impact will be lost if a small standard is planted among tall bush roses.

Standards are not specific varieties, but ordinary bush varieties budded on to a long stem, which makes it possible to plant bush and standard forms of the same variety – say standard and bush forms of 'Iceberg' in an all-white bed. For a less subtle and more dazzling effect, choose a contrasting colour.

Weeping standards are varieties of ramblers. The stems cascade and are sometimes trained over an umbrella-like frame, though many experts do not approve of these and consider

ABOVE: An uncommon variety, 'Centenaire de Lourdes' is a floribunda that makes a spectacular standard.

LEFT: Patio standards are becoming popular, especially for small gardens where space is limited. Here 'Sweet Dream' brings a breath of beauty by the front door – a lovely welcome for visitors.

that the stems look better if allowed to cascade naturally. In either case weeping standards will produce a curtain of colour, with stems that often cascade to ground level. Ground cover roses, such as 'Grouse' and 'Nozomi', are also used to produce weeping standards, and even shrub roses with arching stems, such as 'Ballerina' and 'Canary Bird', can be obtained in this form.

Weeping roses almost always look best as specimen plants in a lawn, where their symmetry and beauty can be fully appreciated.

Patio standards are usually dwarf floribundas on stems about 75 cm (2½ ft) tall, and these look great by the front door or in a light porch, as well as on the patio.

BELOW LEFT: A well-grown weeping standard has evenly spaced shoots all around the head, cascading almost to ground level.

BELOW RIGHT: The rambler 'Excelsa' makes a superb weeping standard that is always an eye-catcher.

BOTTOM RIGHT: 'American Pillar' is more often seen growing over pergolas, but it also makes a pleasing standard.

How Tall?

Standards vary in height. Although different growers may use slightly different terminology and sizes, these are typical stem heights (the actual head may increase the total height):

Miniature standard: 45 cm (1 ½ ft)
Half standard: 75 cm (2 ½ ft)
Patio standard: 75 cm (2 ½ ft)
Full standard: 1 m (3 ft)
Weeping standard:
     1.2–1.5 m (4–5 ft)

PERFECTION IN MINIATURE

Miniatures are tiny, scaled-down roses, perfect for those who enjoy the exquisite beauty of tiny plants, or who simply do not have the space for full-sized roses.

Most miniatures are small versions of hybrid tea and floribunda roses, though a few climbers are also classified as miniature.

Miniatures are widely sold as pot plants, but they are unsuitable for a permanent place indoors. They are best planted in the garden when the initial display is over, but they must first be carefully hardened off. If you are buying miniature roses with the garden in mind, choose those sold for the purpose, whether from a garden centre or by mail order.

As with full-sized roses, some varieties are more vigorous and taller than others: the larger ones may be too big for a miniature rose garden but very suitable for raised beds and other uses.

ABOVE: Miniatures are often sold as pot plants, but they can only be kept indoors for a short period before they begin to deteriorate. Tiny miniatures like this could look lost in a bed outdoors.

While the tiniest varieties grow to only about 15 cm (6 in), most miniatures are 20–30 cm (8–12 in) tall, while the larger ones reach 30–38 cm (12–15 in). A few, such as 'Peek A Boo', border on being a patio rose, and you may find such borderline varieties classed as either miniatures or patio roses in different catalogues.

USING MINIATURE ROSES

A few enthusiasts build rose gardens in miniature, complete with scaled-down beds, paths and lawns. This often appeals to model-makers and rose enthusiasts with little more than a small backyard or balcony. Miniatures are far more versatile than this, however, and they have a role to play even in a large garden.

In a small garden, miniatures and patio roses can replace full-sized versions if the desire is for a collection of many different varieties – though beware of planting a bed with individual specimens of dozens of different roses: plant at least five of one variety to make an impact. A whole bed of one miniature variety will have much more impact than a medley of different ones, as they will probably vary in height and habit as well as colour.

Raised beds, whether on the patio or elsewhere, are the ideal home for miniature roses. They are closer to eye level, and the beauty of their individual flowers can be appreciated.

Miniatures make pleasing outdoor table decorations for, say, a patio table. They can also be used in window boxes, tubs and troughs, but they do not mix well with summer bedding plants, which tend to swamp them. Pack your containers with miniature or patio roses.

LEFT: Beds of miniature roses can be very pleasing, but lots of plants are required to achieve the same kind of impact as far fewer full-sized floribunda roses.

ABOVE: *Try miniatures in pots and containers for the patio.*

LEFT: *Raised beds are ideal for miniature roses, which are thus brought closer to eye level.*

Explore possibilities in the rock garden. To some, a rose will seem alien among true alpines, but in a rock garden where many different kinds of plants are grown, miniature roses will bring summer colour after most traditional rock plants have passed their best. Choose real dwarfs or the taller miniatures according to the space available and the scale of the rock garden.

STANDARDS AND CLIMBERS

Miniature standards are available, but for a general garden display they may not have any more impact than the ordinary bush forms – which are also less expensive. Standards come into their own as part of a miniature version of a full-sized rose garden, planted along with the bush forms.

"Miniature climber" is a potentially misleading term. Although small in comparison with normal climbers, they are not necessarily in scale with the bush forms. In general, they are best regarded as small climbers suitable for the patio or other areas where space is restricted.

ABOVE: *Miniature roses can be planted in the rock garden, where they will bring colour at a time when it is scarce among the alpines.*

LEFT: *Miniature standards are best grown among bush miniatures, where they look in scale and are easily seen.*

POTTED PLEASURES

Do not dismiss the idea of roses as container plants. Pots and tubs enable roses to be grown in parts of the garden that would otherwise be bereft of them, and in some town gardens it is the *only* way it is possible to grow them.

Most kinds of rose can be grown in a container provided it is large enough. Except in the case of miniatures, this means a half-barrel, shrub tub, or large pot with a diameter of *at least* 30 cm (12 in) and preferably 45 cm (18 in). As the rose will remain in its container for many years, it is worth investing in an ornamental container that looks decorative in its own right. It will enhance the beauty of the rose and look more pleasing in winter when the rose is dormant.

Decide on the final position of the container before planting, as once finished it will be very heavy to move.

WHAT TO GROW

Patio roses (dwarf floribundas) are showy and easy to grow, but full-sized floribundas and hybrid teas can be grown if the container is large enough. Unfortunately, the latter look inelegant when dormant and are best positioned where they can be appreciated in summer but are not too dominant in winter. A rose of a pale colour such as white or yellow will show up superbly against a hedge or wall when in flower, while in winter the bare stems will not be too obtrusive. However, hybrid teas would not be a good choice to grow by the front door.

Rather than grow a bush form of a hybrid tea or floribunda, consider a standard. These make impressive container plants and can become useful focal points.

ABOVE: Floribundas like 'The Times Rose' can make imposing container plants, but they must be pruned thoroughly and watered and fed as necessary.

LEFT: Miniatures are some of the best roses for containers. This is 'Sunny Sunblaze'.

BELOW: 'Flower Carpet' is an outstanding patio or ground cover rose. This plant was still in flower in late autumn in its year of planting.

Small patio roses and miniatures can be grown in smaller containers that are easily moved to a less conspicuous spot in the garden for the dormant season.

In general, shrub roses are too large and loose in their growth habit to make perfect container plants, but some of the English roses, such as 'Evelyn', or dainty tea or China roses, are sufficiently compact to be grown in a half-barrel.

Climbers are sometimes planted in large containers, perhaps if they have to climb against a wall where there is no soil in which to plant them. Small climbers, such as 'Warm Welcome' and 'Nozomi', can be planted in free-standing containers supported by a tepee of canes.

Watering and Feeding

Containers will require daily watering at the height of summer, possibly twice a day in very hot weather. This is a job for the cool of evening, when less water will be lost through evaporation.

To maintain vigour in subsequent years after planting, top-dress with bonemeal or work in a rose fertilizer at the rate recommended by the manufacturer each spring.

Supplementary feeding will be necessary for vigorous plants, particularly climbers, and a foliar or liquid feed will be quick-acting and provide the necessary boost. Do not feed after mid-summer, however, as sappy growth that has not ripened fully will be vulnerable to winter frost damage.

LEFT: 'Nozomi' is an extremely versatile rose that takes readily to life in a container. Unless it is trained up a support, it will spread and cascade and completely hide the container in a surprisingly short time. This specimen has been planted only a couple of months yet is already well established in its plastic shrub tub.

BELOW: 'Nozomi' shows its versatility again, this time growing from a half-basket fixed to the house wall. Some other ground cover roses can be grown in a similar way.

BOTTOM: The pure white floribunda 'Iceberg' brings light to a dull corner, and is perfectly happy in its large container.

PLANTING A ROSE IN A CONTAINER

*S*ome roses will do well in containers, but they require careful planting to get them off to a good start and provide conditions that will sustain them in future years.

1 Cover the base of a half-barrel or large pot with stones or gravel for drainage and to provide stability, then part-fill the container with a loam-based potting soil. This will have a better reserve of nutrients and give greater stability than a peat or peat-substitute mixture.

2 Check the planting depth while the rose is still in its container. The top of the root-ball should be about 2.5 cm (1 in) below the rim of the container, to allow for watering.

4 Set the rose in position in the centre of the container and backfill with the potting soil.

3 Ease the rose out of its container and carefully tease out some of the roots to encourage them to grow out into the surrounding soil.

5 Once the correct level has been reached, firm the potting soil to remove any large pockets of air where the roots could dry out.

6 Water the rose thoroughly. To improve its appearance, sprinkle fine gravel, stone chippings or chipped bark over the surface. This will also reduce evaporation from the soil.

Supporting a Climber

To support a climber in a free-standing container, insert about five canes (an odd number looks best), pushing them to the bottom for stability. Tie the tops of the canes together to create a "wigwam", then tie string or plastic-coated wire around the canes in loops about 20 cm (8 in) apart, or in a spiral as shown. Tie in the stems as they grow.

The following climbing and rambling roses are suitable for growing in containers: 'Casino', 'Céline Forestier', 'Climbing Orange Sunblaze', 'Dublin Bay', 'Golden Showers', 'Good as Gold', 'Laura Ford', 'Maigold', 'Nice Day', 'Phyllis Bide', 'Swan Lake', 'Warm Welcome', 'White Cockade'.

RIGHT: With regular feeding and watering, a small climber will send up strong stems that can be trained into a permanent structure around cane supports.

CARE AND CONDITIONING OF CUT ROSES

Whether you are buying roses or cutting them from the garden, always choose those in the very best condition. Reputable florists, supermarkets and flower stalls take pride in their flowers, selling only good-quality blooms and having the knowledge and experience to keep them that way.

If you are cutting roses from the garden, it is best to do this first thing in the morning, when their water content is highest. Cut the flowers at a sharp angle just above a leaf node and be sure not to be so greedy that you rob each bush of all its blooms or destroy its overall appearance! Place the flowers immediately in a bucket of water, where they can have a long drink before you arrange them.

If you are buying roses, make sure they are well wrapped to avoid excess evaporation and to protect their delicate petals. For long journeys it is better to put them in a bucket of water but, if this is impractical, ask the retailer to cover the stem ends with damp paper. As soon as you reach home, give the flowers a long drink in deep tepid water.

Before arranging the flowers, always cut off any foliage that will fall below the water line in the container or vase. Make a long, diagonal cut from the bottom of each stem, as this will provide the maximum area for water intake. Rose stems should never be crushed with a hammer as so many books advocate. Independent research has proved that this method

ABOVE: As a gift, lay a bunch of roses and foliage diagonally on a square of paper and fold around the stems. Tie securely with raffia or ribbon.

destroys the delicate plant cells and makes the stalk less efficient in taking up water; it also encourages the spread of bacterial infection.

Bacteria block the stems and cause the drooping heads so often experienced with shop-bought roses. You can avoid this problem by always using scrupulously clean vases, removing all leaves below the water level and adding commercially formulated flower food. This simple powder contains the correct amount of a mild and completely harmless disinfectant, which inhibits bacterial growth, together with a sugar that

feeds the roses and encourages the flowers to mature and open. If flower food is added to the water it is unnecessary to change it, but it may need topping up in warm weather. Although many people have their own recipes for increasing roses' longevity – lemonade, aspirins, household bleach and so on – flower food is by far the most successful way of keeping roses at their best for longer.

For arrangements using plastic foam, make holes for the rose and other stems with a wooden skewer. If you push the rose stem straight into the foam, particles of foam may become lodged in the base of the stem and prevent good water uptake, causing premature wilting.

If rose heads have wilted, and this may be a result of bacterial infection or an airlock somewhere in the stem, it may be possible to revive them by wrapping them in strong paper and standing the stems in tepid water up to their heads for several hours after first cutting at least 5 cm (2 in) from the end of each stem. If this treatment fails, even more drastic action will be needed and the roses will have to be cut very short in order to perk up their drooping heads.

Finally, there are many theories about rose thorns. Again, research has proved that bacteria may invade the gashes left in the stem when thorns are cut off, so it is better to do this only if the roses are being carried in a bouquet or posy where thorns could prick the hands.

PREPARING ROSES FOR A VASE ARRANGEMENT

1 Always place roses in a bucket of tepid water for a couple of hours after purchase or cutting.

4 If thorns have to be removed because the roses are being used in a bouquet, use sharp scissors to cut them off, but not too close to the stem.

2 After choosing the vase, cut off any leaves that will fall below the water level, as these will rot and stagnate the water.

5 Add a proprietary flower food to the water in the vase to prolong the life of cut flowers and help to keep the vase water clear.

7 Give first aid to wilting flower heads by wrapping them securely in stiff paper and standing them in a large container of tepid water for a few hours.

3 Using a very sharp knife or pair of scissors, cut the stem diagonally to ensure maximum water uptake.

6 It is sometimes possible to revive wilted roses by cutting the stems very short.

DRYING AND STEAMING ROSES

DRYING ROSES

Roses have been dried for as long as they have been cultivated; their petals have been used in potpourri or the whole stems in decorative arrangements when the fresh flowers were scarce. The Elizabethans preserved roses by immersing them completely in dry sand and keeping them warm until all the moisture had been drawn out. In Victorian times, when houses were heated with open coal fires, which shortened the lives of fresh blooms, intricate dried arrangements were painstakingly created and then covered in glass domes to keep them dust-free. These rather tortured, contrived designs have long since lost their appeal in preference for looser, more natural arrangements and contemporary designs using dried flowers have gained a new popularity.

There are three principal ways of drying roses: in the air, in a microwave oven and using a desiccant. The latest commercial method is freeze-drying. This successful technique was originally developed as a means to store penicillin and blood plasma during the Second World War. It requires specialized freezers so it is no use putting a bunch of roses in a domestic model. The process can take up to two weeks and is therefore very expensive but the results are stunning, producing dried roses with all their former intensity of colour and, in some cases, even preserving their perfume. Flowers or bouquets dried by this method can allegedly last for about five years before they start to fade or disintegrate.

Air-drying is the most common method and by far the cheapest as it requires no more than the cost of the roses. This method is best for rosebuds that are just about to open but

BELOW: The easiest way to dry roses is to hang them upside-down in a dark, warm and well ventilated room.

ABOVE: Once the roses are completely dry, carefully strip off the leaves and tie the buds tightly together. Combined with a halo of dried lavender, a small posy in a terracotta pot makes a delightful gift.

DESICCANT-DRYING

Desiccant-drying using silica gel crystals or fine sand may be used for fully open roses.

Silica gel is available from some larger pharmacies.

1 Put 1 cm (½ in) of the crystals or sand in an airtight container and lay the rose-heads face up.

2 Cover very carefully with more sifted desiccant until every part of the flower is concealed. Then tightly seal the container and keep at room temperature for approximately seven to ten days before removing from the desiccant.

still have their bud shape. They need to be hung somewhere warm, dry and dark with good ventilation for a couple of weeks – a large airing-cupboard may be ideal. Stringing them together washing-line-style speeds up the process and prevents any moisture being trapped between the flowers, which may develop into mildew. Once they are completely dry, handle them with care as the stems are very brittle. A tight bunch of rose-buds packed together in a small terracotta pot will give added impact to the now-faded colour of the petals. A gentle blow on the lowest setting of a hair drier usually removes most of any dust.

As the flowers need to fit the radius of the turntable, microwave-drying is suitable only for arrange-ments requiring quite short stems. Lay the flowers on greaseproof paper and put into the microwave oven on the lowest setting. The roses need to be checked every minute to prevent "over-cooking".

STEAMING ROSES

This simple technique can greatly improve the appearance of dried roses which are imported in large boxes with up to 25 bunches per box. Frequently, some or all of the bunches arrive at their destination rather squashed. This process will give them a new lease of life, but take care. Never try to open the very centre of the rose, which is often discoloured. The process also works very well for peonies.

2 Remove the rose from the steam and gently push back the outer petals, one by one. Do not tug at the petals or you will find them coming away in your hand.

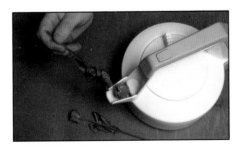

1 Bring a kettle to the boil. Hold the rose by its stem, head down-wards, in the steam for a few seconds, until the outside petals start to waver.

3 If necessary, repeat the steaming process and continue to open the petals, working from the outside towards the centre.

ROSE GALLERY

*T*his gallery of roses contains just a small selection
of the varieties that can be obtained from specialist
rose nurseries and garden centres, and is intended to
be a representative selection of roses new and old. If
you have not planted roses before, use it to help you
decide on the types of roses that appeal to you, but
bear in mind that these are just a few of hundreds of
excellent varieties available for your garden.

RAMBLERS AND CLIMBERS

'ALBERTINE' (RAMBLER)
Introduced in 1921, this is one of the best known of all ramblers, deservedly popular for its heavy scent, prolific flowering and lovely colour. The blooms become untidy as they pass their peak, and the variety is prone to mildew, but it is still an outstanding rose. Height: 4.5 m (15 ft). Spread: 3.5 m (12 ft).

'AMERICAN PILLAR' (RAMBLER)
Introduced in 1902, this used to be a very popular rose. It has fallen out of favour, perhaps because of its single flowers, lack of scent, and susceptibility to mildew. Despite these drawbacks, it is an eye-catching rose for a pillar or pergola, making an outstanding garden feature. Height: 4.5 m (15 ft). Spread: 2.4 m (8 ft).

'BOBBIE JAMES' (RAMBLER)
Introduced in 1961, this versatile but vigorous rambler looks good growing over a large pergola, on a large support at the back of a border, or scrambling into a tree. The cupped, white, semi-double flowers are small but borne in large trusses and sweetly scented. Height: 9 m (30 ft). Spread: 6 m (20 ft).

'CLIMBING ENA HARKNESS' (CLIMBER)
Introduced in 1954, it was a sport (mutation) from the then popular hybrid tea 'Ena Harkness'. It requires coaxing and does best in a warm, sheltered site, but it has the shape and scent of a classic rose. Height: 4.5 m (15 ft). Spread: 2.4 m (8 ft).

'DANSE DU FEU' (CLIMBER)
Introduced in 1954, and by modern standards prone to blackspot, this vivid rose is nevertheless very free-flowering and remains a popular climber. It flowers from summer to autumn, and the blooms are lightly scented. Height: 2.4 m (8 ft). Spread: 2.4 m (8 ft).

'DUBLIN BAY' (CLIMBER)
Introduced in 1976, this is an outstanding climber for a small garden. The lightly scented flowers are produced amid healthy, glossy leaves from summer to autumn. A good choice where a climber that is not too rampant is required. Height: 2.4 m (8 ft). Spread: 2.4 m (8 ft).

PREVIOUS PAGE: Rosa 'Graham Thomas'.

'HANDEL' (CLIMBER)

Introduced in 1965, and a variety valued primarily for its unique colouring, this vigorous rose flowers from mid-summer to autumn. It is only lightly scented, and blackspot may be a problem, but the flowers stand up well to wet weather. Height: 3 m (10 ft). Spread: 2.1 m (7 ft).

'MADAME GRÉGOIRE STAECHELIN' (CLIMBER)

Introduced in 1927, but still grown for its sweetly scented warm pink flowers, borne in profusion in early summer. It flowers only once, but at its peak the display is superb, and there are large showy hips to redden in autumn. Height: 6 m (20 ft). Spread: 3.5 m (12 ft).

'MAIGOLD' (CLIMBER)

Introduced in 1954 and still widely planted, this is an outstanding rose valued for its disease resistance and early flowering (usually by late spring). Unfortunately it does not continue to flower through the summer. The leaves are leathery and glossy. Height: 2.4 m (8 ft). Spread: 2.4 m (8 ft).

'PARKDIREKTOR RIGGERS' (CLIMBER)

Introduced in 1957 but highly regarded for its disease resistance and long flowering season. The semi-double flowers are only lightly scented, but are produced from summer into autumn. It has glossy dark green leaves. Height: 3.5 m (12 ft). Spread: 2.4 m (8 ft).

'PINK PERPÉTUE' (CLIMBER)

Introduced in 1965, and a variety with exceedingly beautiful blooms, borne from summer to autumn, its spreading habit makes it suitable for covering a wall. The blooms are only lightly scented, and the leaves may succumb to rust. Height: 3 m (10 ft). Spread: 2.4 m (8 ft).

'WHITE COCKADE' (CLIMBER)

Introduced in 1969, it is still valued for its perfectly shaped flowers. The blooms are only slightly scented, but produced almost continuously from summer to autumn. It is a good choice for a container or for growing on a short pillar. Height: 2.1 m (7 ft). Spread: 1.5 m (5 ft).

Floribunda (Cluster-Flowered) Roses

'Anisley Dickson'
Introduced in 1985, and named after the breeder's wife – an indication of a good rose. It is a fine bedding rose and makes a pleasing hedge. It is only slightly fragrant, but with abundant foliage. Height: 1 m (3 ft). Spread: 60 cm (2 ft).

'Anna Livia'
Introduced in 1988, this free-flowering variety is ideal for bedding, with fragrant, hybrid-tea-shaped blooms. Height: 75 cm (2½ ft). Spread: 60 cm (2 ft).

'Bright Smile'
Introduced in 1980, this is a fitting name for a cheerful yellow rose which flowers early and produces a good succession of bloom. Its low height and bushy growth make it suitable for the front of a border or as a low hedge. It shows good disease resistance. Slight fragrance. Height: 60 cm (2 ft). Spread: 45 cm (1½ ft).

'Buck's Fizz'
Introduced in 1990. Though grown primarily for its soft orange colour, the blooms are also fragrant. Height: 1 m (3 ft). Spread: 60 cm (2 ft).

'Champagne Cocktail'
Introduced in 1985, this showy rose is very decorative, free-flowering and shows very good disease resistance. It makes a colourful bed, and is also an attractive cut flower, with a strong scent for floribundas. Height: 1 m (3 ft). Spread: 60 cm (2 ft).

'Coventry Cathedral'
Introduced in 1973, the colour makes this a real eye-catcher in full flower. Unfortunately it is susceptible to blackspot. Height: 75 cm (2½ ft). Spread: 60 cm (2 ft).

'ELIZABETH OF GLAMIS'
Introduced in 1964, and once a very popular rose with a good fragrance. By modern standards it is prone to diseases and dieback, but it is lovely when grown in good soil. Height: 75 cm (2½ ft). Spread: 60 cm (2 ft).

'EVELYN FISON'
Introduced in 1962, it became very popular and is still highly regarded. The colour is strong and does not fade even in the hottest sun. Slight fragrance. Height: 1 m (3 ft). Spread: 60 cm (2 ft).

'EYE PAINT'
Introduced in 1976, this is an exceptionally showy plant that stands out even when viewed across the garden. Its flowers are borne in great profusion, on a vigorous bush that grows larger than most floribundas. It looks at home in a shrub border, and makes an excellent informal hedge. There is no fragrance. Height: 1.2 m (4 ft). Spread: 75 cm (2½ ft).

'GLAD TIDINGS'
Introduced in 1989, when it was voted Rose of the Year. Good for beds, borders or an informal hedge, but only slightly fragrant. The flowers are produced in profusion and continue to flower over a long period. Height: 75 cm (2½ ft). Spread: 60 cm (2 ft).

'HANNAH GORDON'
Introduced in 1983. The delicately coloured flowers are well set off by the glossy bronze-green foliage. Height: 1 m (3 ft). Spread: 60 cm (2 ft).

'HARVEST FAYRE'
Introduced in 1990, when it won the Rose of the Year award. A bushy grower with large clusters of flowers late into the season. Some fragrance. Height: 1 m (3 ft). Spread: 60 cm (2 ft).

'ICEBERG'
Introduced in 1958, this is still one of the best white floribundas. The large flower clusters are borne in profusion, making it excellent for a massed effect or an informal hedge. It is also known by the name 'Schneewittchen'. Height: 1.2 m (4 ft). Spread: 60 cm (2 ft).

'MASQUERADE'
Introduced in 1949, and still one of the most easily identified roses. Although seldom planted now, its multicoloured effect still has appeal. There is only slight fragrance, and it requires regular dead-heading to keep the flowers coming. Height: 1 m (3 ft). Spread: 60 cm (2 ft).

'MATANGI'
Introduced in 1974, this is an eye-catching rose that produces a large profusion of flowers throughout the growing season, set off against glossy foliage. It is only slightly fragrant but it makes an excellent bedding rose and shows good disease resistance. Height: 75 cm (2½ ft). Spread: 60 cm (2 ft).

'MEMENTO'
Introduced in 1978. A very free-flowering rose with large trusses of blooms that continue to be produced throughout the season. The flowers are very weather-resistant and the plant's disease resistance is good too. There is only a trace of scent. Height: 75 cm (2 ½ ft). Spread: 60 cm (2 ft).

'MOUNTBATTEN'
Introduced in 1982, when it was Rose of the Year. The large, scented flowers show up well against the shiny foliage which is abundantly produced and persists well into winter. This variety is useful as an isolated shrub as well as in a rose bed or as an informal hedge. Height: 1 m (3 ft). Spread: 75 cm (2½ ft).

'QUAKER STAR'
Introduced in 1991. The medium-sized flowers remain beautifully shaped at all stages, from bud to fully open bloom. Only slightly fragrant. Height: 1 m (3 ft). Spread: 60 cm (2 ft).

'SHEILA'S PERFUME'
Introduced in 1985. Good perfumes are
not common among the floribundas, but
this one is very fragrant and it has won
awards for its scent. The flowers have long,
straight stems and are ideal for cutting.
Height: 1 m (3 ft). Spread: 60 cm (2 ft).

'STRAWBERRY ICE'
Introduced in 1979. The blooms have the
kind of delightful colour combination that
makes this rose difficult to ignore. It
makes a good show in the garden and is
great for cutting. Height: 1 m (3 ft).
Spread: 60 cm (2 ft).

'TANGO'
Introduced in 1989. The strikingly
coloured flowers are borne in great
profusion, but are only slightly fragrant.
An award-winning rose that deserves a
place in the garden. Height: 75 cm (2½
ft). Spread: 60 cm (2 ft).

'THE TIMES ROSE'
Introduced in 1984/5, this award-winning variety has a depth of colour that makes it an
impressive bedding rose. The dark green foliage increases the impression of substance.
Fragrance is only slight. Height: 1 m (3 ft). Spread: 60 cm (2 ft).

'VALENTINE HEART'
Introduced in 1990, this variety is aptly
named as it has a romantic appearance
and there is the bonus of a strong
perfume. The blooms are very weather-
tolerant, and the variety has justifiably
won several awards. Height: 1 m (3 ft).
Spread: 60 cm (2 ft).

GROUND COVER ROSES

'FERDY'

Introduced in 1984. An attractive shrub with arching growth. Its height means it is only suitable for ground cover in a large garden. Height: 1.2 m (4 ft). Spread: 1 m (3 ft).

'FIONA'

Introduced in 1979. A shrubby rose with flower sprays borne throughout the summer, set against plentiful dark green glossy foliage. Height: 60 cm (2 ft). Spread: 1.5 m (5 ft).

'GROUSE'

Introduced in 1984. A prostrate shrub suitable for a bank or other large area. The flowers are fragrant and the foliage disease-resistant. Height: 30 cm (1 ft). Spread: 3 m (10 ft).

'HERTFORDSHIRE'

Introduced in 1991. A ground-hugging shrub with a profusion of bloom over a very long flowering period. Height: 30 cm (1 ft). Spread: 1 m (3 ft).

'NOZOMI'

Introduced in 1968, and bred in Japan. It is a very versatile plant with many uses – it will sometimes be found classified as a miniature climber. Although the flowers are not bright, they are borne in profusion in mid-summer, and may go on appearing into the autumn. Height: 30 cm (1 ft). Spread: 1.2 m (4 ft).

'PINK BELLS'

Introduced in 1980, it has arching growth with dark green shiny foliage that acts as a pleasing backdrop for the pink flowers. The slightly fragrant flowers are borne in mid- and late summer. Its height means it is only suitable for ground cover in a large garden. Height: 75 cm (2½ ft). Spread: 1.2 m (4 ft).

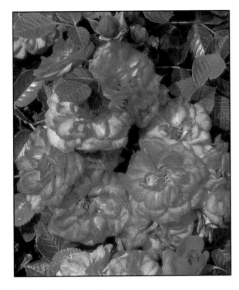

'RED BELLS'

Introduced in 1983. A charming rose, similar to 'Pink Bells' (see previous page) apart from its colour. Height: 75 cm (2½ ft). Spread: 1.2 m (4 ft).

'RED MAX GRAF'

Introduced in 1984. A vigorous shrub with arching growth. It has one main flush of flowers in summer, but they are carried in profusion over dark green foliage. A good ground cover rose for a bank. Height: 45 cm (1½ ft). Spread: 1.5 m (5 ft).

'ROSY CUSHION'

Introduced in 1979. Good repeat flowering, and vigorous spreading growth with dense glossy foliage, but its height makes it unsuitable for areas requiring compact ground cover. Height: 1 m (3 ft). Spread: 1.2 m (4 ft).

'SNOW CARPET'

Introduced in 1980. A distinctive prostrate rose with creeping stems and a mass of tiny foliage to help smother weeds. Flowers for most of the summer and into the autumn. Height: 23 cm (9 in). Spread: 1 m (3 ft).

'THE FAIRY'

Introduced in 1932. A dwarf polyantha rose and one of the oldest ground cover roses, but still useful where there is space for it. Height: 75 cm (2½ ft). Spread: 1.2 m (4 ft).

HYBRID TEA (LARGE-FLOWERED) ROSES

'ALEXANDER'

Introduced in 1972, and still one of the best within its colour range. The long stems also make it a popular choice for cutting, and its size is suitable for hedging. Fragrance is only slight, but it holds many international awards. Height: 1.5 m (5 ft). Spread: 60 cm (2 ft).

'BLUE MOON'

Introduced in 1964, and popular because of its unusual colour and distinctive name, though it is a lilac-blue and not a true blue. The flowers are nicely pointed and have a good scent. It has reasonably good disease resistance. Height: 1 m (3 ft). Spread: 60 cm (2 ft).

'DAWN CHORUS'

Introduced in 1993, when its strong colour and good shape helped it win Rose of the Year and Breeder's Choice awards in that year. A free-flowering vigorous plant, it is ideal for rose beds, but its fragrance is only moderate. Height: 1 m (3 ft). Spread: 60 cm (2 ft).

'FULTON MACKAY'

Introduced in 1988, since when it has proved itself to be an excellent all-round rose. It has a sharp, spicy scent, weather resistance is good and the leaves are large and glossy. Height: 1 m (3 ft). Spread: 60 cm (2 ft).

'INGRID BERGMAN'

Introduced in 1986, and grown mainly for its strong colour and classic flower shape, though its fragrance is only light. The growth is strong and upright, with dark green glossy foliage, and it makes a good bedding rose. Height: 1 m (3 ft). Spread: 75 cm (2½ ft).

'JUST JOEY'

Introduced in 1973, but still grown for its distinctive colouring. The blooms are often large and it is always an eye-catching rose, but with only a slight scent. Its bushy growth makes it a good choice for a rose bed. Height: 75 cm (2½ ft). Spread: 60 cm (2 ft).

'KEEPSAKE'
Introduced in 1981. An attractive colour, good shape and sweet scent are its main attributes. It is a vigorous grower, with plenty of foliage. Height: 1.2 m (4 ft). Spread: 60 cm (2 ft).

'LOVELY LADY'
Introduced in 1986. A shapely, full-petalled rose with a pleasing fragrance. It looks especially good in a bed of a single variety. Height: 75 cm (2½ ft). Spread: 60 cm (2 ft).

'PAINTED MOON'
Introduced in 1989. A stunning colour combination, eye-catching in the garden or as a cut flower. Fragrance is only slight, but its cheerful colouring compensates. Height: 75 cm (2½ ft). Spread: 60 cm (2 ft).

'PAUL SHIRVILLE'
Introduced in 1983, and one of the best pink varieties. Plentiful blooms and a strong scent are coupled with vigorous growth and plenty of foliage. It has won many international awards. Height: 1 m (3 ft). Spread: 60 cm (2 ft).

'PEACE'
Introduced in 1945, and one of the most famous roses of all time. There are now better varieties, but it is still a beautiful rose and many grow it because it is such a familiar old favourite. Little scent. Height: 1.2 m (4 ft). Spread: 75 cm (2½ ft).

'PEAUDOUCE'
Introduced in 1985, and now established as a leading variety in its colour range. An excellent rose for cutting, but its fragrance is only slight. Height: 1 m (3 ft). Spread: 60 cm (2 ft).

'PICCADILLY'
Introduced in 1960, and highly regarded at the time, it is still a popular bicolour variety. It comes into bloom early and is free-flowering. Its drawbacks are its slight fragrance and blooms that quickly open wide and lose their shape. Height: 1 m (3 ft). Spread: 60 cm (2 ft).

'POLAR STAR'
Introduced in 1982, and Rose of the Year in 1985. The well-shaped blooms are carried on vigorous shoots, and the dark green foliage acts as a pleasing backdrop for the white flowers. It has a spicy perfume, and good weather-resistance. Height: 1 m (3 ft). Spread: 60 cm (2 ft).

'PRIMA BALLERINA'
Introduced in 1957. Well-shaped blooms with a strong and typical rose scent. Vigorous growth, but it is unfortunately susceptible to mildew and flowering is not always prolific. Height: 1 m (3 ft). Spread: 60 cm (2 ft).

'PRINCESS ROYAL'
Introduced in 1992. One of the best hybrid teas for shape and colour, and with the bonus of a pleasant spicy fragrance. Strong, bushy growth. Height: 1 m (3 ft). Spread: 60 cm (2 ft).

'ROSEMARY HARKNESS'
Introduced in 1985. A popular choice because of its fragrance, and excellent for cuttings as well as bedding. Well-branched vigorous growth makes it a reliable garden rose. Height: 1 m (3 ft). Spread: 60 cm (2 ft).

'ROYAL WILLIAM'
Introduced in 1987, in which year it was voted Rose of the Year. It is currently one of the best of its colour with a heady scent, and the sturdy bushes have strong, healthy foliage. Height: 1 m (3 ft). Spread: 60 cm (2 ft).

'RUBY WEDDING'
Introduced in 1979. Not an exceptional rose, but popular as an anniversary gift because of its name. The fragrance is only slight, but the rose makes a pleasing display in small groups in a border. Height: 1 m (3 ft). Spread: 60 cm (2 ft).

'SAVOY HOTEL'
Introduced in 1989. It has perfectly shaped blooms, is excellent as a cut flower with its strong stems and plentiful foliage, and a first-rate hybrid tea for bedding. Moderate scent. Height: 1 m (3 ft). Spread: 60 cm (2 ft).

'SILVER JUBILEE'
Introduced in 1978, and still one of the best hybrid teas for general planting. It flowers freely and the vigorous, bushy plants are very disease-resistant. It has won many awards. Light fragrance. Height: 1 m (3 ft). Spread: 60 cm (2 ft).

'SIMBA'
Introduced in 1981. One of the most perfectly formed yellow hybrid teas, it makes an excellent cut flower. Slight fragrance. The plants are bushy and it is one of the best yellows for bedding. Height: 75 cm (2½ ft). Spread: 60 cm (2 ft).

'TROIKA'
Introduced in 1971, and sometimes known as 'Royal Dane'. An excellent all-round rose, good for bedding, excellent for cuttings, and large enough to exhibit, with good weather-tolerance and disease-resistance. Height: 1 m (3 ft). Spread: 60 cm (2 ft).

'TYNWALD'
Introduced in 1979. Large flowers on sturdy stems with lush, disease-resistant foliage. Moderate fragrance. Height: 1 m (3 ft). Spread: 60 cm (2 ft).

Miniature Roses

'ANGELA RIPPON'
Introduced in 1978. A bushy, leafy plant, it makes a good choice for the edge of a border as well as raised beds and containers. Because of its height, it is classified as a patio rose in some catalogues. Height: 45 cm (1½ ft). Spread: 30 cm (1 ft).

'BABY MASQUERADE'
Introduced in 1966, and deservedly still a favourite. It grows freely and blooms continuously over a long period. It looks better planted in groups than as an individual plant. Height: 30 cm (1 ft). Spread: 23 cm (9 in).

'BUSH BABY'
Introduced in 1986. It has bushy growth with plenty of foliage, and is pleasing both as a massed group or grown as an individual plant. Height: 30 cm (1 ft). Spread: 23 cm (9 in).

'CINDERELLA'
Introduced in 1953. The white flowers tend to have a touch of pink, especially in cool weather. The bushy plants have disease-resistant foliage. Height: 30 cm (1 ft). Spread: 23 cm (9 in).

'ORANGE SUNBLAZE'
Introduced in 1981, and still widely grown for its large and long-lasting flowers. Bushy growth, and free-flowering, but unfortunately there is no scent. Height: 38 cm (15 in). Spread: 23 cm (9 in).

'RED ACE'
Introduced in 1982. Perfectly formed flowers, a strong colour, and compact growth make this a highly desirable miniature. Height: 30 cm (1 ft). Spread: 23 cm (9 in).

(left) **'RED SUNBLAZE'**
Introduced in 1980. A vivid rose that makes a great splash of colour despite its small size. It repeat-flowers well. Height: 38 cm (15 in). Spread: 23 cm (9 in).

(right) **'STACEY SUE'**
Introduced in 1976. A pretty miniature that looks well proportioned. Bushy growth. Height: 38 cm (15 in). Spread: 30 cm (1 ft).

PATIO ROSES

'ANNA FORD'
Introduced in 1980, and one of the
leading patio varieties, having amassed
many top international awards. A good
choice for an edging as well as a patio bed
or pot, but with little fragrance. Height:
45 cm (1½ ft). Spread: 45 cm (1½ ft).

'CONSERVATION'
Introduced in 1988. An eye-catching rose
with flowers well set off by abundant
bright, glossy foliage. Although not
strongly fragrant, it does have a pleasant
scent. Height: 45 cm (1½ ft).
Spread: 45 cm (1½ ft).

'DRUMMER BOY'
Introduced in 1987, and an outstanding
variety for brilliance of colour and
profusion of flowers. It has little scent.
Plant in small groups towards the front of
a border, or as a low edging or hedge, as
well as in containers. Height: 45 cm
(1½ft). Spread: 45 cm (1½ ft).

'GENTLE TOUCH'
Introduced in 1986, when it was voted
Rose of the Year – one of the first patio
roses to win the title. The dainty blooms
are produced in profusion, sometimes
covering the strong and sturdy plants.
Little scent. Height: 60 cm (2 ft).
Spread: 45 cm (1½ ft).

'HAKUUN'
Introduced in 1962, and still one of the
finest whites. The name means "white
cloud", which accurately describes the
appearance of the plant in full bloom.
There is only a slight fragrance. Height:
60 cm (2 ft). Spread: 45 cm (1½ ft).

'PEEK A BOO'
Introduced in 1981. Prolific in bloom, this
little rose is a good choice to fill in gaps
towards the front of a border, or to grow
in a tub. Height: 60 cm (2 ft).
Spread: 45 cm (1½ ft).

'RAY OF SUNSHINE'
Introduced in 1989. An unfading yellow, with a backing of small, shiny foliage. Quick to repeat-flower, but only a slight scent. Height: 45 cm (1½ ft). Spread: 45 cm (1½ ft).

'ROBIN REDBREAST'
Introduced in 1984. An excellent low-growing plant that could be used instead of summer bedding. It is spectacular planted *en masse*, and ideal for edging a border. Height: 45 cm (1½ ft). Spread: 45 cm (1½ ft).

'ROSABELL'
Introduced in 1988, this is a charming variety with flowers shaped like those of an old rose. It flowers prolifically and there is a slight scent. Height: 45 cm (1½ ft). Spread: 45 cm (1½ ft).

'RUGUL'
Introduced in 1973. Grown mainly for its bright yellow colour, which does not fade readily in hot sun. Good repeat-flowering is also a feature, but there is little scent. It is sometimes listed as a miniature. Height: 45 cm (1½ ft). Spread: 45 cm (1½ ft).

'SWEET MAGIC'
Introduced in 1987, when it won the Rose of the Year award. Beautifully formed flowers with a light fragrance, on bushes well clothed with foliage. Height: 45 cm (1½ ft). Spread: 45 cm (1½ ft).

'TOP MARKS'
Introduced in 1992, when it won the highest score ever at that time in the Rose of the Year trials, as well as other awards in several countries. Its strong points are a dazzling colour and prolific blooming. It also has good disease-resistance but is only lightly scented. Height: 45 cm (1½ ft). Spread: 45 cm (1½ ft).

SHRUB ROSES

'ANDERSONII'
A *Rosa canina* hybrid, but the flowers are larger than those of the dog rose. They are sweetly scented and followed by showy red hips in autumn. Height: 2.1 m (7 ft). Spread: 2.4 m (8 ft).

'BELLE DE CRÉCY'
A gallica rose bred before 1829, with quartered-rosette, sweetly scented flowers, produced in abundance in mid-summer. It is considered to be one of the best gallicas, but has a laxer habit than most and may require some support. Height: 1.2 m (4 ft). Spread: 1 m (3 ft).

'BLAIRII NUMBER TWO'
A Bourbon rose raised in 1845. Untrained it will grow into an arching shrub, but its vigour makes it suitable for growing on a pyramid or pergola or against a wall, and it is often catalogued as a climber. The sweetly scented flowers are produced mainly in mid-summer. Height against a wall: 4.5 m (15 ft). Spread: 2.4 m (8 ft).

'BUFF BEAUTY'
A hybrid musk, sometimes classified as a modern shrub rose, probably bred before 1939. The sweetly scented flowers are carried in two flushes, the autumn flowering being less profuse. Mildew may be a problem in late summer. Height: 1.5 m (5 ft). Spread: 1.5 m (5 ft).

'CÉCILE BRÜNNER'
A polyantha rose sometimes classified as a China rose, introduced in 1881. It produces its delicately scented flowers from summer to autumn. It used also to be known as 'The Sweetheart Rose'. A climbing form is often planted. Height: 1 m (3 ft). Spread: 1 m (3 ft).

'CÉLESTE'
An alba rose whose date of introduction is uncertain, though it is certainly very old. The flowers are sweetly scented and carried on lax, spreading stems. There is a bonus of red hips in autumn. It is sometimes called 'Celestial'. Height: 1.8 m (6 ft). Spread: 1.8 m (6 ft).

'CHAPEAU DE NAPOLÉON'

A centifolia rose bred in the 1820s and now more correctly known as *Rosa x centifolia* 'Cristata'. Its richly scented flowers open flat and are sometimes quartered. The name 'Chapeau de Napoléon' refers to the heavily mossed buds which look like tricorn hats. Height: 1.5 m (5 ft). Spread: 1.2 m (4 ft).

'CHARLES DE MILLS'

A gallica rose of unknown parentage and date of introduction. It makes a compact shrub with moderately scented crimson flowers, which fade into purple and grey tones as they mature. The stems are slender and may require staking. Height: 1.2 m (4 ft). Spread: 1 m (3 ft).

'COMPLICATA'

A gallica rose of uncertain origin, and untypical of most gallicas. The single flowers are sweetly scented and produced in abundance in summer. The leaves are matt greyish-green. It can be used as a rambler among other shrubs in a wild garden or trained on a pillar. Height: 2.4 m (8 ft). Spread: 2.4 m (8 ft).

'CONSTANCE SPRY'

A modern shrub rose, sometimes classified as an 'English' rose, introduced in 1961. The peony-like flowers are heavily scented, but it flowers only once in summer. Untrained, it makes a lax shrub, but it can be grown as a climber on a pillar. Height: 1.8 m (6 ft). Spread: 1.8 m (6 ft).

'FÉLICITÉ PARMENTIER'

An alba rose, known since about 1834, that grows as a compact shrub. Its highly scented flowers are borne in mid-summer, the densely packed petals fading almost to white in hot sun and reflexing to form a ball-shape. It is one of the daintiest albas, suitable for a small garden. Height: 1.2 m (4 ft). Spread: 1.2 m (4 ft).

'GRAHAM THOMAS'

A modern shrub or 'English' rose, raised in 1983. The pleasantly scented flowers are produced in succession from summer to autumn. Named in honour of the great English rosarian Graham Stuart Thomas. Height: 1.2 m (4 ft). Spread: 1.2 m (4 ft).

'GRUSS AN AACHEN'

A polyantha rose sometimes classified as a
modern rose or as a cluster-flowered
bush, bred around 1909. The flowers are
delicately scented and carried in clusters
from summer to autumn. Its long
flowering season and low growth habit
make it an outstanding rose. Height: 1 m
(3 ft). Spread: 1 m (3 ft).

'ISPAHAN'

A damask rose first recorded in 1832 but
probably much older; it may be Persian in
origin. The flowers are richly scented, but
there is only the one flush in summer.
However, it has a longer flowering period
than most other damasks and is in bloom
for up to six weeks. Height: 1.5 m (5 ft).
Spread: 1.2 m (4 ft).

'KÖNIGIN VON DÄNEMARK'

An alba rose, produced in 1826, that
makes an elegant bush with richly scented
flowers in summer. It has a long flowering
season – up to six weeks – and the blooms
have good resistance to wet weather. The
variety is sometimes sold as 'Queen of
Denmark'. Height: 1.5 m (5 ft).
Spread: 1.2 m (4 ft).

'L. D. BRAITHWAITE'

A modern shrub rose introduced in 1988,
and one of the best for continuity of
flower, with top quality blooms and a rich
fragrance. Height: 1.2 m (4 ft).
Spread: 1.2 m (4 ft).

'MADAME HARDY'

A damask rose dating from 1832. The
strongly scented flowers are borne in
profusion in summer. This is generally
considered to be one of the most sumptuous of old roses, though the flowers may
be spoilt by rain. Height: 1.5 m (5 ft).
Spread: 1.5 m (5 ft).

ROSA 'ALBA MAXIMA'

An alba rose dating from at least the 15th
century. The somewhat untidy flowers are
very fragrant, and followed by red hips. It
is otherwise known as the 'Great Double
White', 'Jacobite' or 'Cheshire Rose',
while some consider it to be the 'White
Rose of York'. Height: 1.8 m (6 ft).
Spread: 1.5 m (5 ft).

ROSA RUGOSA

A species rose with distinctive wrinkled leaves and bright pink single flowers, followed in autumn by very large rounded hips. It is a good choice for a rose hedge, especially in coastal areas. Height: 1.8 m (6 ft). Spread: 1.5 m (5 ft).

ROSA XANTHINA 'CANARY BIRD'

A form of wild rose of uncertain origin but assumed to have been introduced after 1907. It flowers early, in late spring, and though the flowers are single they are large and conspicuous, with fern-like leaves as a foil. It is sometimes available as a standard. Height: 2.1 m (7 ft). Spread: 2.1 m (7 ft).

'ROSERAIE DE L'HAŸ'

A rugosa hybrid introduced in 1901. The heavily scented flowers are borne continuously through summer and into autumn. The bright green leaves are heavily crinkled. This weather-resistant rose makes an excellent hedge. Height: 2.1 m (7 ft). Spread: 2.1 m (7 ft).

'STANWELL PERPETUAL'

A Scotch rose, raised in 1838, with sweetly scented flowers produced almost continuously throughout the summer. The leaves are grey-green. It makes a good hedge. Height: 1.5 m (5 ft). Spread: 1.5 m (5 ft).

'WILLIAM LOBB'

A moss rose introduced in 1855, with highly scented flowers that open from heavily "mossed" buds. This is a vigorous rose that makes a sprawling upright shrub. It can be trained as a short climber on a pillar or against a wall. Height: 1.8 m (6 ft). Spread: 1.8 m (6 ft).

Sources and Suppliers

UK

Rose Societies

The Royal National Rose Society
contact The Secretary
The Royal National Rose Society
Chiswell Green
St Albans
Herts AL2 3NR
Tel: 01727 850461

British Rose Growers
  Association
303 Mile End Road
Colchester
Essex
CO4 5EA

Rose Growers
(including old roses, personal shoppers and mail order)

David Austin Roses
Bowling Green Lane
Albrighton
Wolverhampton WV7 3HB
Tel: 01902 373931

Le Grice Roses
Norwich Road
North Walsham
Norfolk NR28 0DR
Tel: 01692 402591

Peter Beales Roses
London Road
Attleborough
Norfolk NR17 1AY
Tel: 01953 454707

Cottage Garden Roses
Woodlands House
Stretton
near Stafford ST19 9LG
Tel: 01785 840217

Essential Oil Suppliers
(shops and mail order)

Neal's Yard Remedies
5 Golden Cross
Cornmarket Street
Oxford OX1 3EU
Tel: 01865 245436

Culpeper Ltd
Hadstock Road
Linton
Cambridge
CB1 6NJ
Tel: 01440 788196

Dried roses
(personal shoppers and mail order)

The Hop Shop
Castle Farm
Shoreham
Sevenoaks
Kent TN14 7UB
Tel: 01959 523219

US

Rose Societies

American Rose Society
Box 300000
Shreveport, LA 711390
Tel: (318) 938 5402

Heritage Roses Foundation
Mr. Charles A. Walker Jr.
1512 Gorman St
Raleigh, NC 27606

American Horticultural Society
7931 East Boulevard Drive
Alexandria, VA 22308
Tel: (703) 768 5700

Rose Growers (including mail order suppliers)

Armstrong Roses
P O Box 4220
Huntington Station, NY 11746
Tel: (800) 321 6640

Lowe's Own-root Roses
6 Sheffield Road
Nashua, NH 03062
Tel: (603) 888 2214

Jackson and Perkins
1 Rose Lane
Medford, OR 97501
Tel: (800) USA-ROSE

Natural Beauty Ingredients

The Body Shop
45 Horse Hill Road
Cedar Knolls, NY 07927-2014
Tel: (800) 541 2535

Kiehl's
109 Third Avenue
New York, NY 10002
Tel: (212) 677 3171

Lorann Oils
P O Box 22009
Lansing, MI 48909-2009
Tel: (800) 248 1302

Dried roses (shops and mail order)

Dody Lyness Co.
7336 Berry Hill Drive
Polos Verdes Peninsula, CA 90274
Tel: (310) 377 7040

Gailann's Floral Catalog
821 W. Atlantic Street
Branson, MO 65616

Nature's Finest
P O Box 10311, Dept. CSS
Burke, VA 22009

AUSTRALIA

Rose Societies

National Rose Society
271B Belmore Road
North Balwyn, Vic 3104
Tel: (03) 9857 9656

Rose Society in Victoria
P. O. Box 1004
Blackburn North Vic 3130
Tel: (03) 9877 4301

Rose Society of NSW
299 Malton Road
North Epping NSW 2121
Tel: (02) 869 7516

Queensland Rose Society Inc.
GPO Box 1866
Brisbane Qld 4001
Tel: (07) 814 4714

Rose Society of South Australia
29 Columbia Crescent
Modbury North SA 5092
Tel: (002) 663 366

Rose Society of Tasmania
RSD 146 Cradoc Hill Road
Cradoc Hill Tas 7109
Tel: (002) 458 6452

Rose Society of W.A.
33 Lord Street
Bentley WA 6102
Tel: (09) 458 6452

Rose Growers

The Perfumed Garden
895 Derril Road
Moorooduc
Victoria 3933

Swane's Nursery
490 Galston Road
Dural
NSW 2158
Tel: (02) 651 1322

Doyles Rose Farm
1389 Waterford Tambourine Road
Logan Village
QLD 4207
Tel: (07) 5546 8216

Brundrett & Sons (Roses) Pty Ltd.
Brundrett Road
Narre Warren North
Victoria 3804
Tel: (03) 9596 8742

Dried roses

Hedgerow Flowers
177 King William Road
Hyde Park
SA 5061
Tel: (08) 373 4779

Roses Only
Shop 12, Chifley Plaza
Chifley Square
Sydney NSW 2000
Tel: (02) 232 4499

The Gardener's Book
  Service
211 Bay Street
Brighton
Victoria 3186
Tel: (03) 9596 8742

$\mathcal{I}$NDEX